Illustrated Index to Traditional American Quilt patterns

Susan Winter Mills

ARCO PUBLISHING, INC.
NEW YORK

To Sally and Stephen

Special thanks to Joe Giardinelli
for stressing the importance of detail

Published by Arco Publishing, Inc.
219 Park Avenue South, New York, N.Y. 10003

Copyright © 1980 by Susan Winter Mills

Printed in the United States of America

Library of Congress Cataloging in Publication Data

Mills, Susan Winter.
   Illustrated index to traditional American quilt patterns.

   Includes index.
   1. Quilting—United States—Patterns.   I. Title.
TT835.M54   745.4′6   79-17147

ISBN 0-668-04777-1   Library Edition
ISBN 0-668-04782-8   Paper Edition

FOREWORD

Favorite of the Peruvians, Wind Power of the Osages, Chinese 10,000 Perfections, Pure Symbol of the Right Doctrine, Battle Ax of Thor, Catch Me If You Can, Heart's Seal, Mound Builders—all names for one quilt pattern; scraps of folk poetry for the pieced-work folk art that, nurtured by necessity, flourished in pre-industrial America.

Quiltmakers were prodigiously inventive—710 quilt designs are compiled herein. They showed a remarkable sense of design and an intuitive grasp of geometrics. As many of the more popular designs spread with the settling of the nation and were repropagated in new soil, they sprang up with new names; the homogenization of language by national media was still far down the road.

My intention when I began compiling patterns was to piece together a reference tool for my own quiltmaking—something to thumb through, like a catalog, a method more conducive to inspiration than going through many books.

At first, the name for each pattern was just that—a name. After poring through the sources and finding the same pattern with different names, their profusion and poetry caught my attention. As I go through the pages now, the names delight me as much as the patterns.

Quilts warmed the Bible Belt: Tents of Armageddon, Job's Tears, Garden of Eden, Ecclesiastical.

Some names are memorials to the birth of the nation and history in the making: Burgoyne Surrounded, Underground Railroad, Sherman's March, Trail of the Covered Wagon, and Free Trade Block.

More mundane events were part of the naming. We can imagine a quiltmaker coming up with Climbing Rose after a satisfying day in the garden, or an accident in the kitchen resulting in Broken Dishes.

Individuals were honored in the naming, too: Martha Washington Star, Barbara Frietchie Star, Lincoln's Platform, and Tippecanoe and Tyler Too.

Many whimsical names were evoked by the patterns: Duck's Foot in the Mud, Pickle Dish, Drunkard's Path, and Wild Goose Chase.

Sister's Choice, Granny's Garden, Aunt Eliza's Star, Mother's Fancy Star, and Baby Bunting all reflect the importance of family; Always Friends, Nextdoor Neighbor, and Friendship Chain echo the warmth of companionship.

To put a practical face on it, collecting as many names as possible is the only sensible way to index patterns that may be known by different names in adjacent counties. In laying out the book, it was necessary to choose one "main" name for each pattern as they were arranged in sections, with secondary names for the pattern listed below the primary name. All names are included in the index to facilitate a pattern search by the reader. If the name for a quilt pattern is the object of the search, the patterns have been arranged in sections according, more or less, to the most prevalent geometric figure. (Some patterns were difficult to classify—they could easily have fallen as well into one classification as another—so I clenched my teeth and surrendered to pure arbitrariness.) After deciding what shape—triangle, square, circle, star, or combination—is predominant in your quilt, you need only thumb through that section until you recognize the pattern.

Since quilt patterns depend on the juxtaposition of light and dark fabric to bring out the design, the illustrations in this book are rendered in black and white. A quiltmaker can find a pattern he or she likes, count the shades therein, assign corresponding shades of fabric, and be assured that the quilt he makes will be a faithful rendering of the pattern.

With many patterns, using different color schemes can cause a subject-field shift or otherwise completely change the aspect of the quilt, making it hard to apprehend how it is put together. Like a blueprint, renderings of patterns in black and white bring up the details relevant to construction.

The patterns were drafted on a five-to-an-inch grid. Overlaying patterns with tracing paper with the same grid provides a unit measure for the pattern. Dividing the projected dimensions of the quilt by the number of units will indicate the size of individual blocks and pieces of the block.

Templates can then be cut to the appropriate sizes and used to trace the pieces on fabric. I cut about ¼ inch beyond and stitch on top of the traced line.

Because of their strong graphic sense, quilt patterns may be adapted for use in many areas of arts and crafts. (Z-Cross contains four figures identical to the NBC-TV logo.) Designs can also be utilized in other textile crafts such as weaving, needlepoint, and embroidery.

After I sent these patterns to the publisher, an article I wrote for my hometown paper prompted a letter from a reader with a query about and sketches of two patterns. One was among the 710 compiled here, but the other was not. I realized that the book will probably generate enough new sources and patterns to provide a diversion for many years to come.

CONTENTS

FOREWORD	iii
STARS	1
TRIANGLES	29
CIRCLES	53
COMBINATIONS	63
SQUARES (RECTANGLES, OCTAGONS, HEXAGONS, DIAMONDS)	97
BIBLIOGRAPHY	118
INDEX OF NAMES	118

Stars

Alice's Favorite

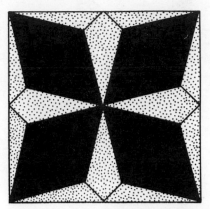

Arkansas Traveller
Travel Star

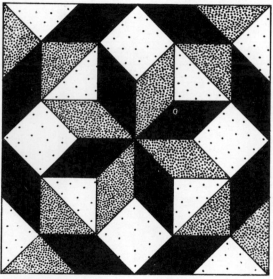

All Hallows

Aunt Eliza's Star

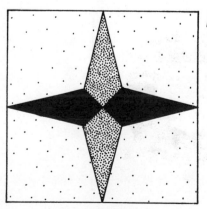

Arkansas Snowflake
  Four-Point
  Job's Troubles, Var. 2
  Kite
  Snowball, Var. 3

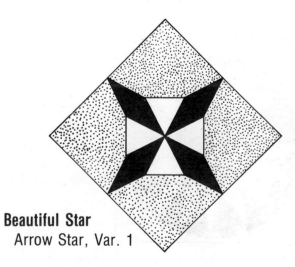

Beautiful Star
  Arrow Star, Var. 1

Blazing Star Variation 1

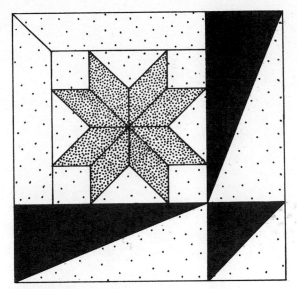

Bouquet in a Fan

Blazing Star Variation 2
Lemon Star, Var. 3

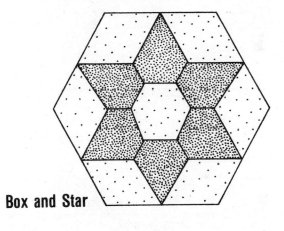

Box and Star

Blazing Sun

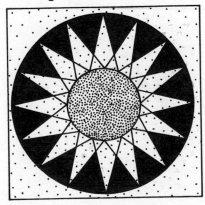

Caesar's Crown

California Star Variation 1

Carpenter's Wheel Variation 2

California Star Variation 2

Chained Star
Brunswick Star, Var. 1
Rolling Star, Var. 3

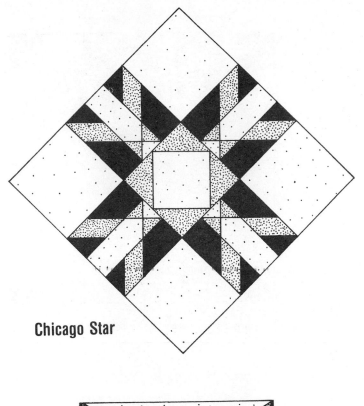

Chicago Star

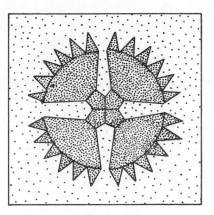

Chips and Whetstones
Variation 1

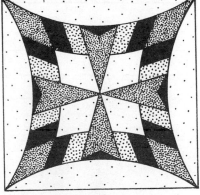

Chimney Swallows

Chips and Whetstones
Variation 2

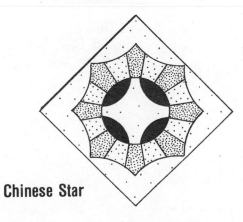

Chinese Star

Chips and Whetstones
Variation 3

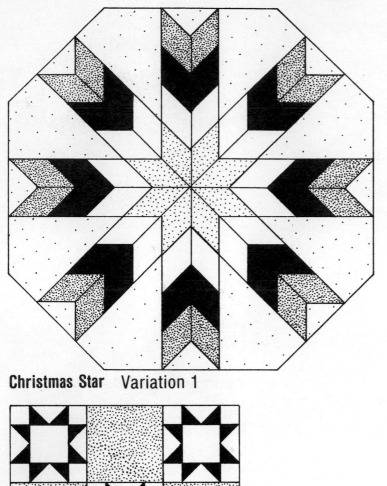

Christmas Star Variation 1

Columbia Star
Star and Blocks

Cluster of Stars

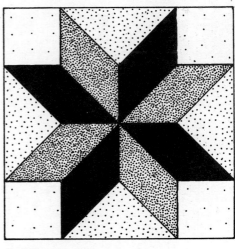

Columns

Columbia Puzzle

Diamond Star
Variation 1

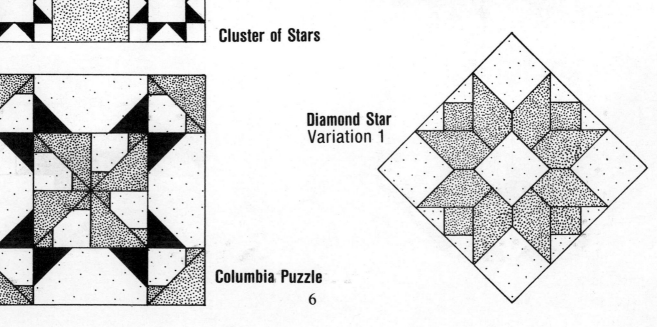

Diamond Star Variation 2

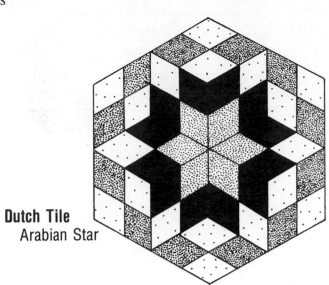

Dutch Tile
Arabian Star

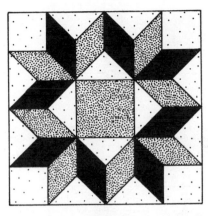

Dove at the Window

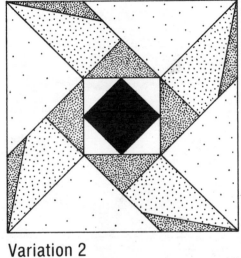

Eccentric Star Variation 2

Dutch Rose
Octagonal Star, Var. 1

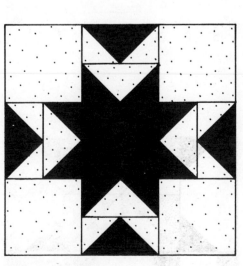

Eight-Pointed Star Variation 2

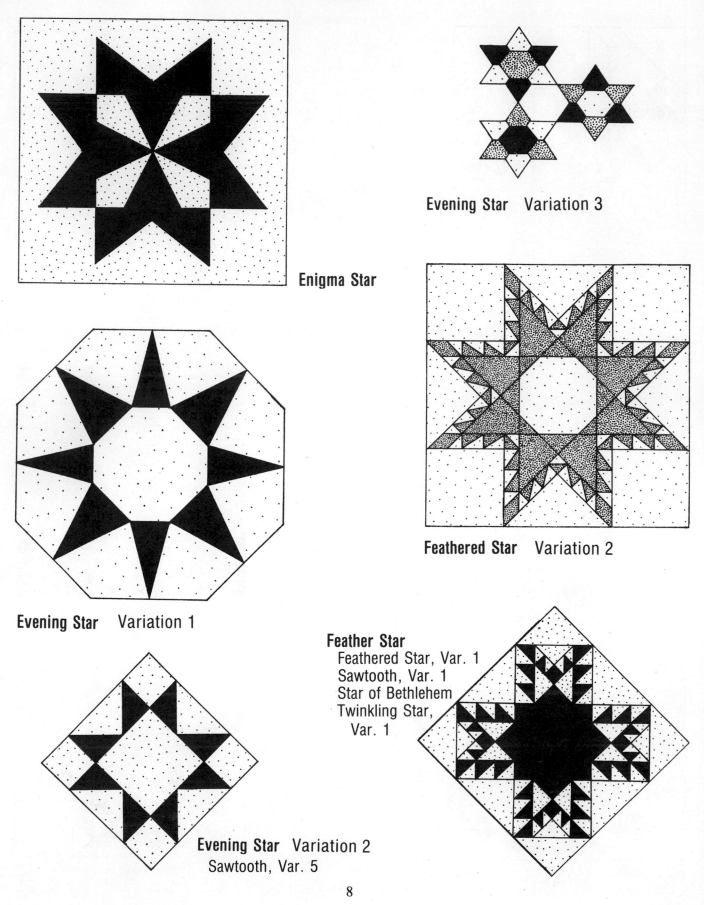

Enigma Star

Evening Star   Variation 3

Feathered Star   Variation 2

Evening Star   Variation 1

Feather Star
Feathered Star, Var. 1
Sawtooth, Var. 1
Star of Bethlehem
Twinkling Star,
Var. 1

Evening Star   Variation 2
Sawtooth, Var. 5

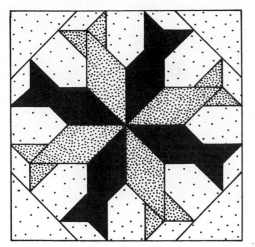

Fish Block
Goldfish

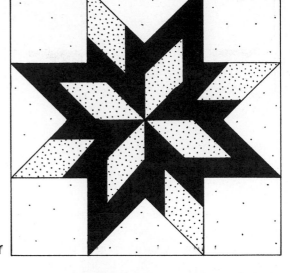

Flying Bat
Polaris Star

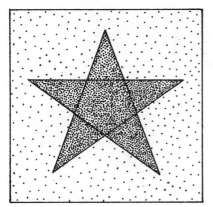

Five-Pointed Star

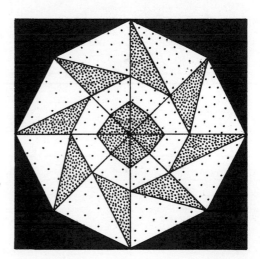

Flying Saucer

Flower Star Variation 1

Flying Swallow
Circling Swallows
Falling Star
Flying Star

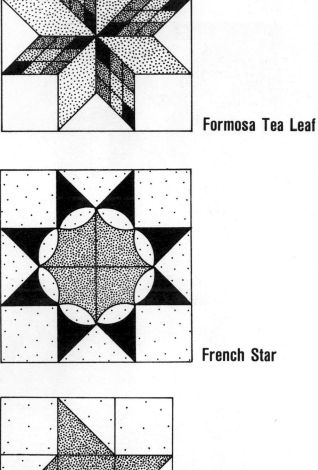

Formosa Tea Leaf

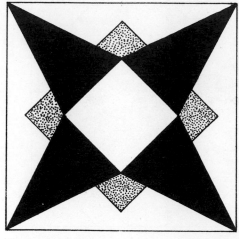

Geometric Star

French Star

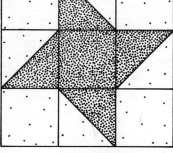

Friendship Star
Variation 1

Georgetown Circle   Variation 2

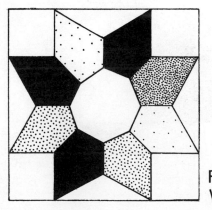

Friendship Star
Variation 2

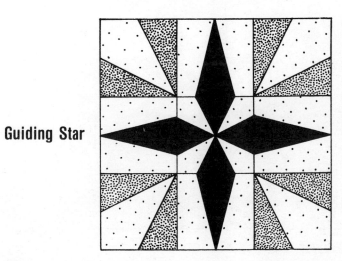

Guiding Star

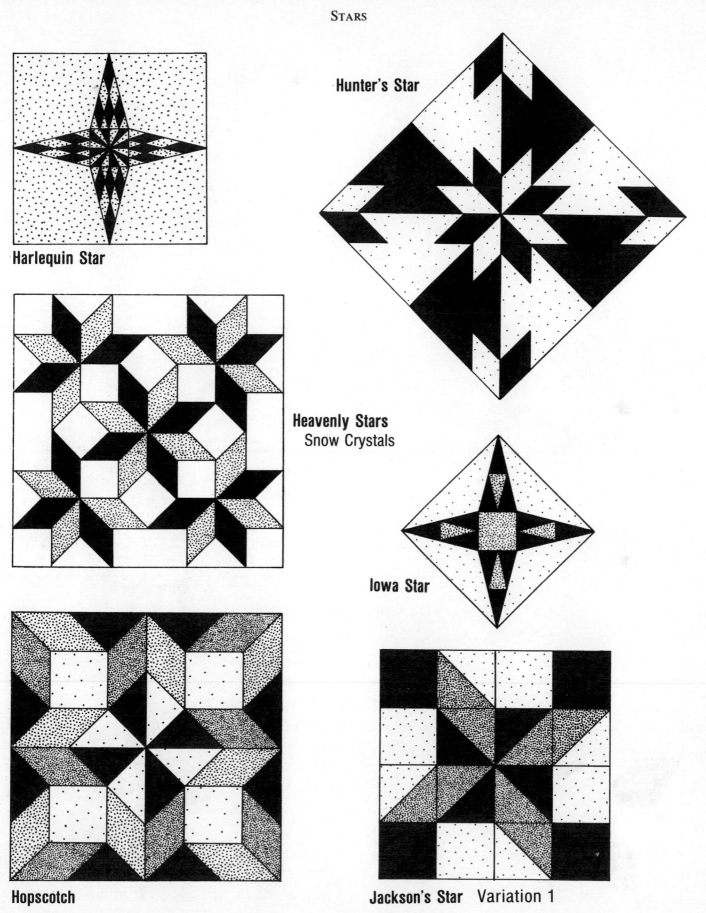

Harlequin Star

Hunter's Star

Heavenly Stars
Snow Crystals

Iowa Star

Hopscotch

Jackson's Star Variation 1

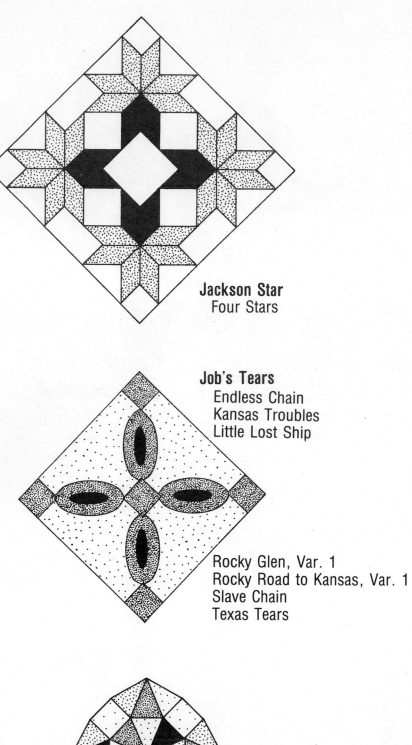

Jackson Star
Four Stars

Key West Star

Job's Tears
Endless Chain
Kansas Troubles
Little Lost Ship

Rocky Glen, Var. 1
Rocky Road to Kansas, Var. 1
Slave Chain
Texas Tears

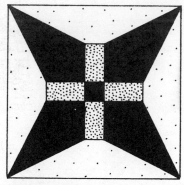

King David's Crown
Variation 1

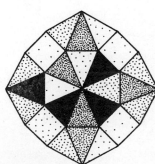

Kaleidoscope Variation 1

King's Star Variation 1

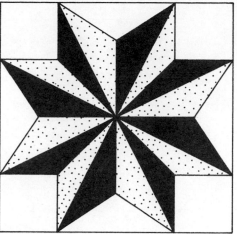

Le Moyne Star   Variation 2
Divided Star
Lemon Star, Var. 2
Star of LeMoine, Var. 2
Star of LeMoyne, Var. 2

Lazy Daisy   Variation 2

Liberty Star

Light and Shadows

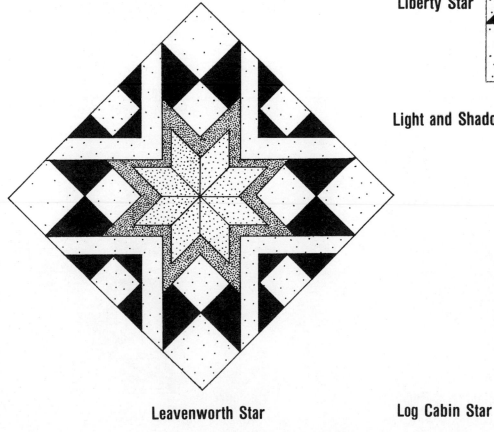

Leavenworth Star

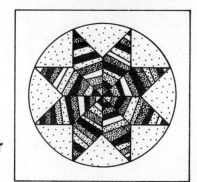

Log Cabin Star

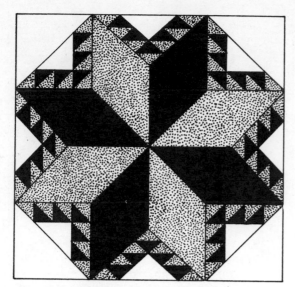

Lucinda's Star

Martha Washington Star

Many-pointed Star

Mexican Rose
Mexican Star, Var. 1

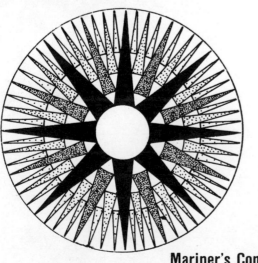

Mariner's Compass
Rising Sun, Var. 1

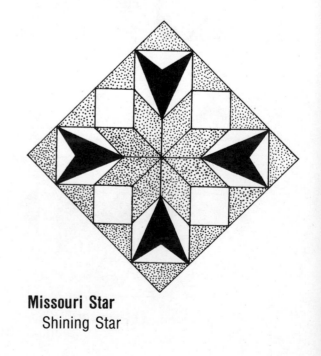

Missouri Star
Shining Star

Modern Star

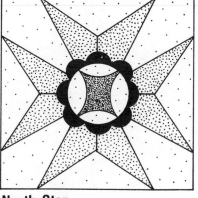

Morning Star   Variation 3

Northern Lights
Blazing Star, Var. 3
Four-Pointed Star
Star, Var. 2

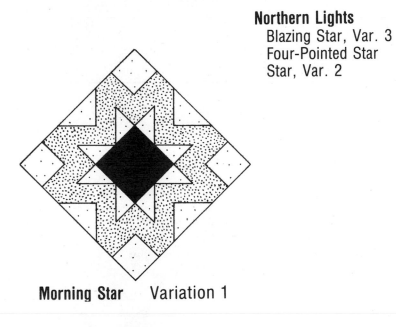

Morning Star   Variation 1

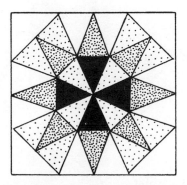

Morning Star   Variation 2

North Star
Star Tulip, Var. 2

Northumberland Star   Variation 2

Odd Star

Odd Fellows' Cross   Variation 1

Ohio Star   Variation 1
Lone Star, Var. 1
Old Tippecanoe and Tyler Too
Variable Star

Odd Fellows' Cross   Variation 2

Ohio Star   Variation 2
Eastern Star, Var. 1
Eight-Point Star
Lone Star, Var. 2
Lucky Star
Shoofly, Var. 2
Texas
Tippecanoe and Tyler Too

Oklahoma Star
Rising Sun, Var. 2

Ozark Star
Ozark Diamond

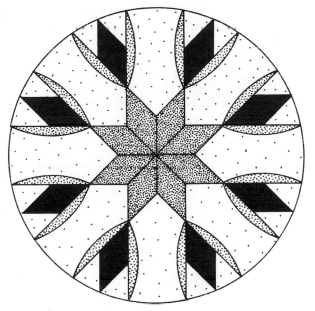

Olive's Yellow Tulip

Patty's Star

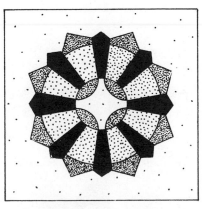

Oriental Star   Variation 1

Persian Star

Pieced Star Variation 1
Pierced Star

Pointing Star

Philippines

Pontiac Star

18

Purple Cross

Prairie Queen
Variation 2

Prairie Star
Harvest Star
Harvest Sun
Ship's Wheel

Queen of the May

Ring Around the Star
Rolling Star, Var. 2
Star and Chains

19

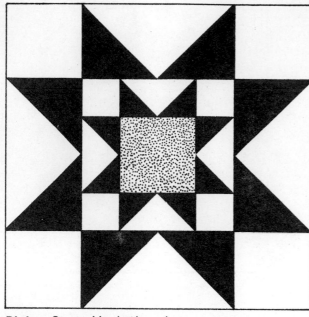

Rising Star Variation 1
Stars and Squares

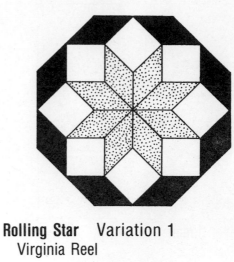

Rolling Star Variation 1
Virginia Reel

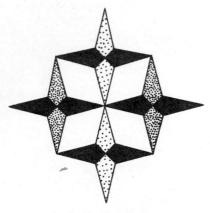

Rock Garden

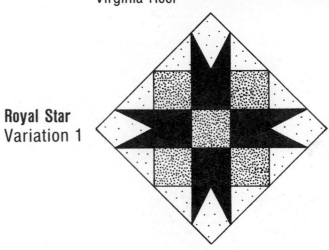

Royal Star
Variation 1

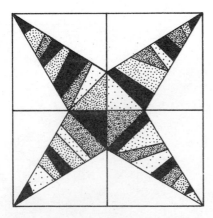

Rocky Road to Kansas Variation 2

Royal Star Variation 2

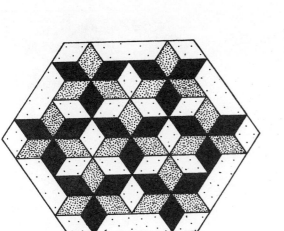

Seven Sisters
Evening Star, Var. 4

Slashed Star
Sunflower

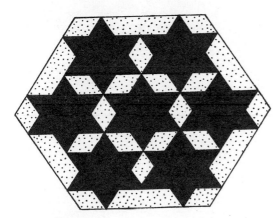

Seven Stars
Boutonniere

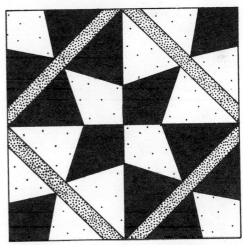

Small Business

Sky Rocket

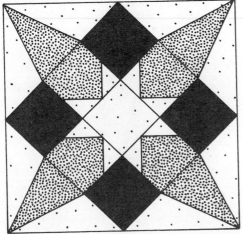

Spiderweb
Variation 2

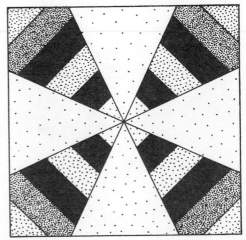

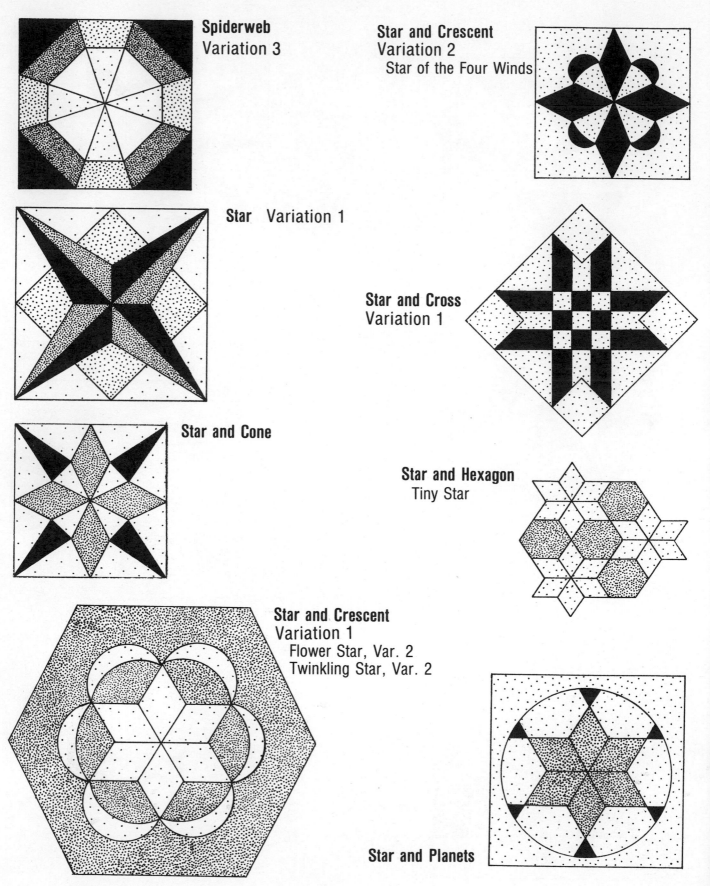

Spiderweb
Variation 3

Star and Crescent
Variation 2
   Star of the Four Winds

Star Variation 1

Star and Cross
Variation 1

Star and Cone

Star and Hexagon
   Tiny Star

Star and Crescent
Variation 1
   Flower Star, Var. 2
   Twinkling Star, Var. 2

Star and Planets

22

Star Flower
Variation 2

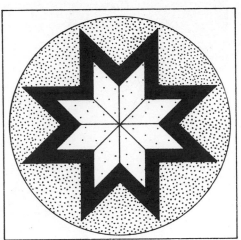

Star of Hope
Variation 2

Starlight   Variation 1

Star of Le Moyne   Variation 1
  Brunswick Star, Var. 2
  Eight-Pointed Star,
    Var. 1
  Lemon Star, Var. 1
  LeMoyne Star, Var. 1
  Star of the East, Var. 1
  Star of LeMoine, Var. 1

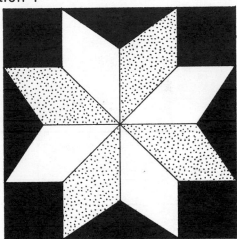

Starlight
Variation 2

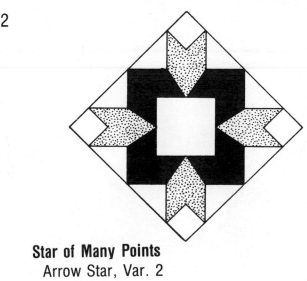

Star of Many Points
Arrow Star, Var. 2

Star of North Carolina
North Carolina Star

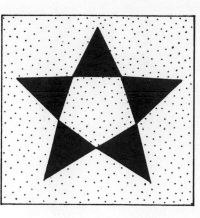

Star of the West
Variation 2

Star of the East   Variation 3
Silver and Gold

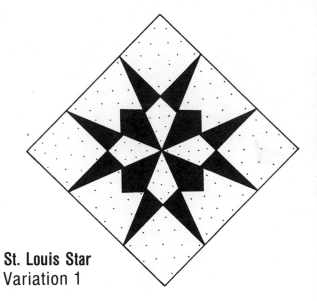

St. Louis Star
Variation 1

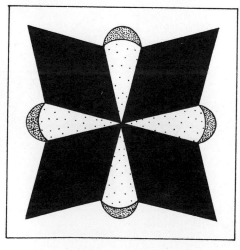

Star of the West
Variation 1
    Compass, Var. 1
    Four Birds
    Four Winds
    King's Star, Var. 2

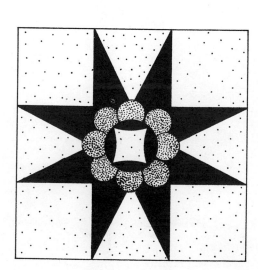

Star Tulip
Variation 1

Sunburst
Variation 1

Star Within a Star
 Carpenter's Wheel, Var. 1
 Double Star
 Star of the East, Var. 2

String Quilt

Sunburst Variation 2

Sunbeam

Sunburst Variation 3

25

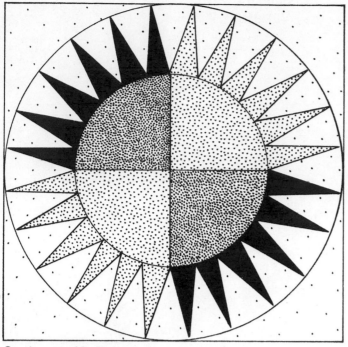

Sunburst   Variation 4

Swallows in a Window

Tennessee Star

Tangled Cobwebs

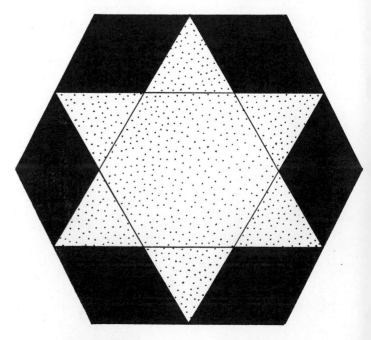

Texas Star

Union Star

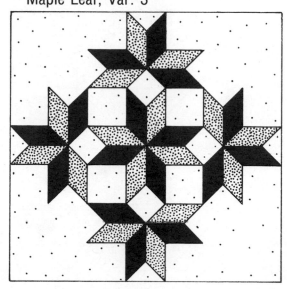

Yankee Pride
Maple Leaf, Var. 3

Virginia Star
    Eastern Star, Var. 2
    Star upon Stars
    Virginia's Star

SUPPLEMENT

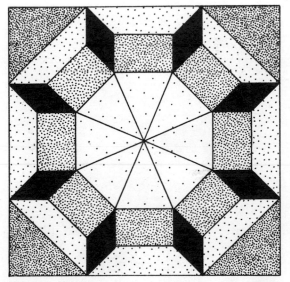

Castle Wall

World Without End
    Amethyst
    Golden Wedding Ring
    Windmill Star

Dolly Madison's Star

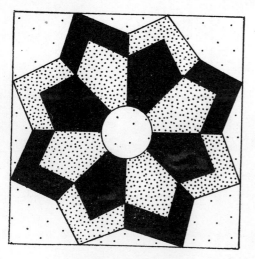

Eight-Pointed Star Variation 3

Triangles

Aircraft

Barbara Frietchie Star
Star Puzzle

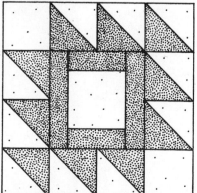

Album
Variation 4

Barn Raising

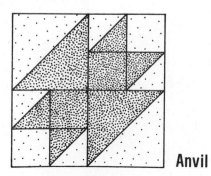

Album
Variation 5

Barrister's Block
Lawyer's Puzzle

Anvil

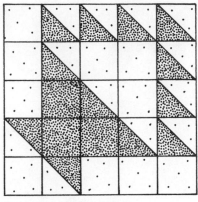

Basket of Triangles
Fruit Basket, Var. 2

Birds in Air
Variation 3

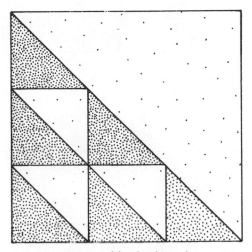

Birds in Air   Variation 1
Flying Birds
Flying Geese, Var. 1
Flock of Geese

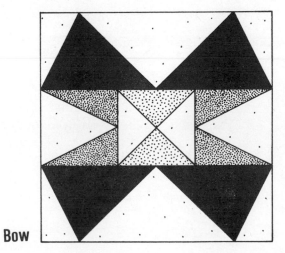

Blindman's Fancy

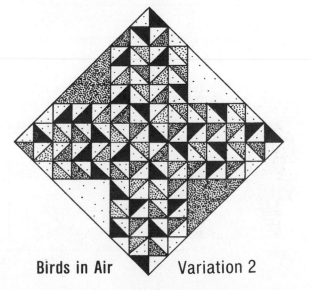

Birds in Air   Variation 2

Bow

Boxes
Variation 2

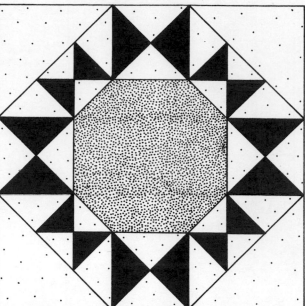

Buttons and Bows
Wheel of Fortune, Var. 3

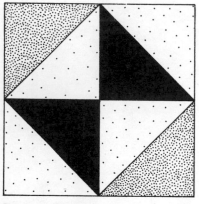

Broken Dishes

Cactus Flower

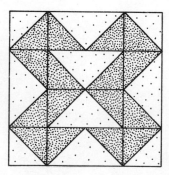

Brown Goose
Brown
Devil's Claws, Var. 1
Double Z
Grey Goose

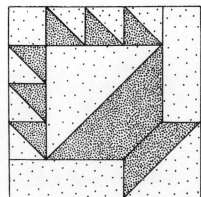

Cakestand

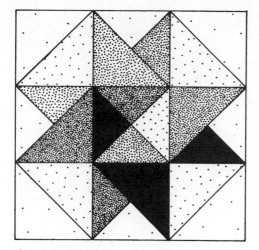

Card Trick

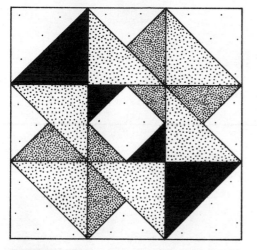

Castle in Air

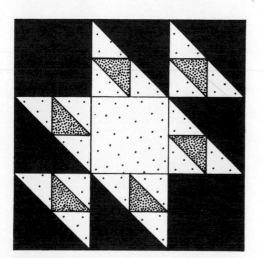

Cat's Cradle

Century
Variation 2

Cherry Basket Variation 1
Flower Basket

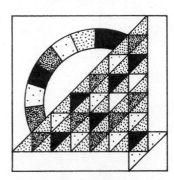

Cherry Basket
Variation 2

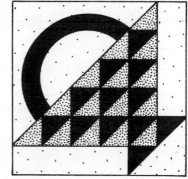

Christmas Tree
Tree of Life, Var. 3

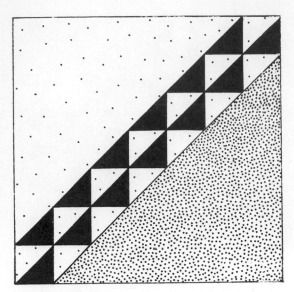

City Square
London Square

Crazy Ann Variation 1
Follow the Leader
Twist and Turn

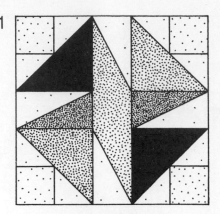

Cross
Variation 1

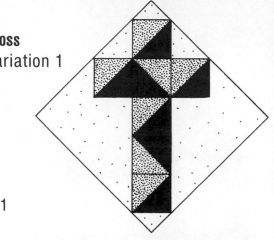

Corn and Beans
Variation 2
    Duck and Duckling
    Handy Andy, Var. 4
    Hen and Chickens, Var. 1
    Shoofly, Var. 4

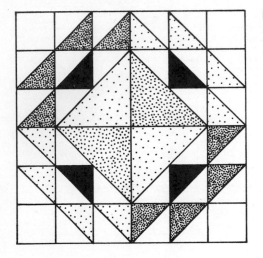

Crossed Canoes
Tippecanoe

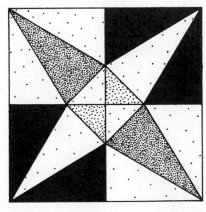

Crosses and Losses
    Double X, Var. 2
    Fox and Geese
    Old Maid's Puzzle
    X

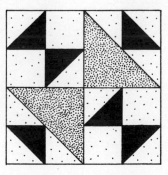

Cotton Reel

34

Double Pyramid

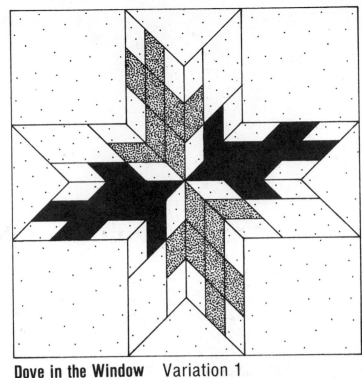

Dove in the Window   Variation 1

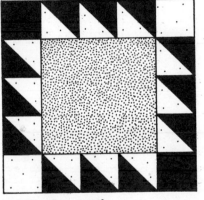

Double Sawtooth

Duck and Ducklings
   Corn and Beans, Var. 1
   Handy Andy, Var. 5
   Hens and Chickens, Var. 1
   Shoofly, Var. 3
   Wild Goose Chase, Var. 2

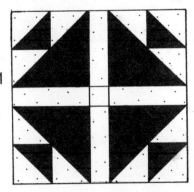

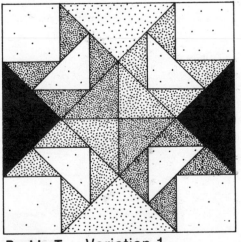

Double T   Variation 1

Dutchman's Puzzle
   Dutch Windmill

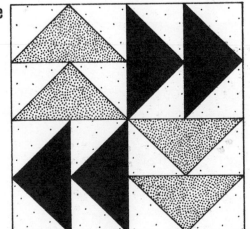

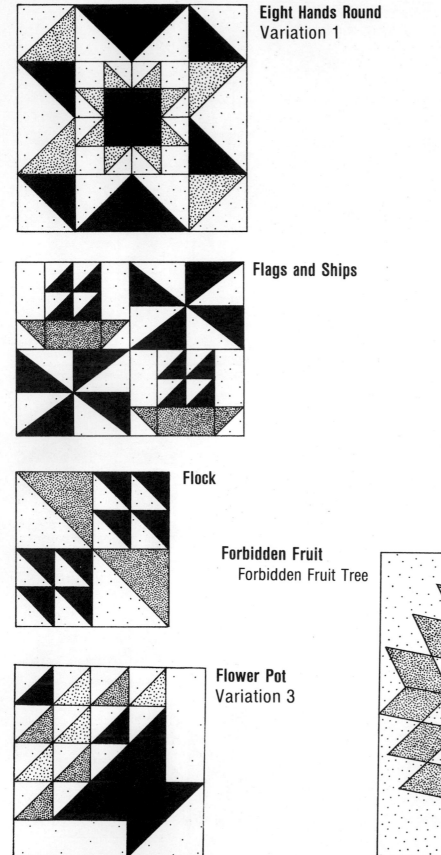

Eight Hands Round
Variation 1

Flags and Ships

Flock

Forbidden Fruit
   Forbidden Fruit Tree

Flower Pot
Variation 3

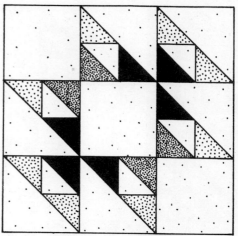

Flying Bird

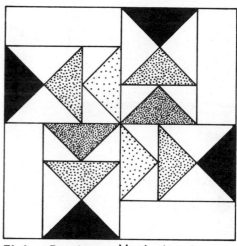

Flying Dutchman Variation 3

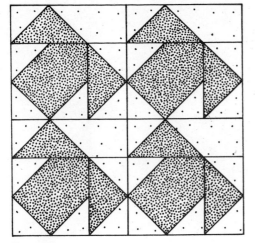

Four Ts
　　Mixed T

Geese in Flight
　　Battlegrounds
　　Indian Trails, Var. 2
　　Rambling Road, Var. 2
　　Soldiers March
　　Storm at Sea, Var. 3

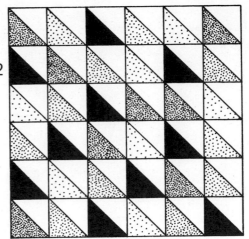

Four X

Georgetown Circles

Fruit Basket　Variation 1

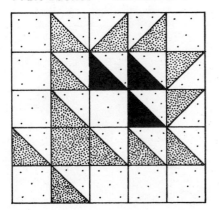

Golden Stairs

Goose in the Pond
Variation 1

Gretchen

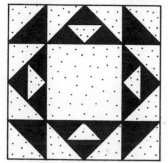

Grandmother's Favorite

Handy Andy Variation 1
Gentleman's Fancy

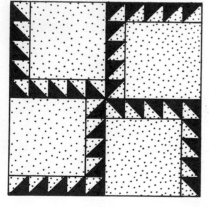

Grandmother's Pinwheel

Hill and Valley

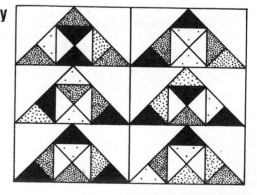

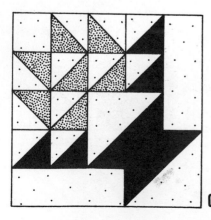

Grape Basket

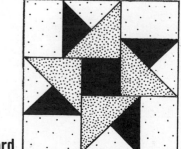

Hope of Hartford

38

Hovering Birds

Ice Cream Bowl

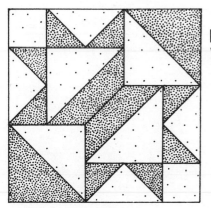

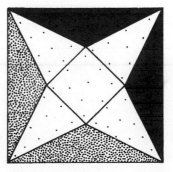

Indian Trails
Variation 1

Bear's Paw, Var. 2
Climbing Rose
Flying Dutchman, Var. 2
Forest Path
Irish Puzzle
Kansas Trouble, Var. 1
North Wind, Var. 1
Old Maid's Ramble, Var. 1
Prickly Pear, Var. 2

Rambling Road, Var. 1
Rambling Rose
Storm at Sea, Var. 1
Tangled Tares
Weather Vane, Var. 1
Winding Walk

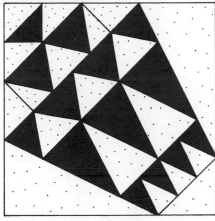

Indian Meadows
Variation 2
    Queen Charlotte's Crown, Var. 2

Kaleidoscope
Variation 2

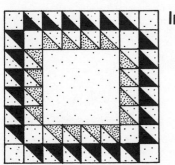

Indian Plumes

Kaleidoscope
Variation 3

39

Kansas Trouble Variation 2

Lost Ships
 Lady of the Lake, Var. 2
 Rockly Glen, Var. 2

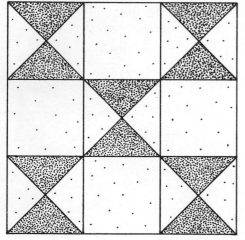

Letter X
 Clown's Choice
 Flying X

Maltese Cross
Variation 1

Maryland Beauty

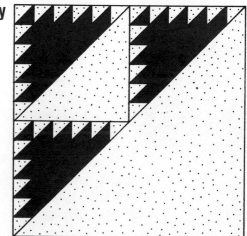

Lightning Strips
 Chevron
 Rail Fence
 Snake Fence, Var. 1
 Streak of Lightning
 Zigzag, Var. 1
 1,000 Pyramids

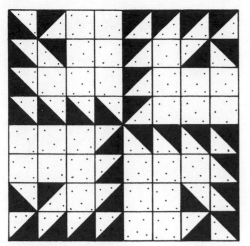

Merry Go Round

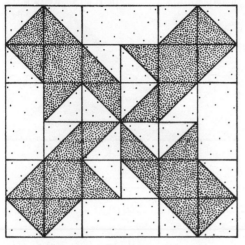

Mrs. Morgan's Choice

New York Beauty
Variation 1

New York Beauty Variation 2
Rocky Mountain Road

Next-door Neighbor

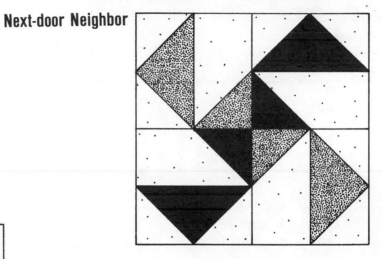

Night and Day

41

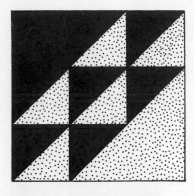

North Wind
Variation 2

Odd Fellows' Chain

Ocean Waves
Variation 1

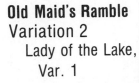

Old Maid's Ramble
Variation 2
   Lady of the Lake,
    Var. 1

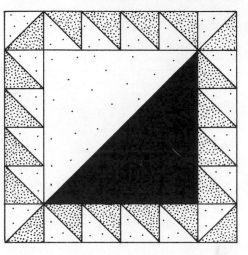

Ocean Waves
Variation 2

Old Maid's Ramble Variation 3
   Crimson Rambler
   Rambler
   Spring Beauty

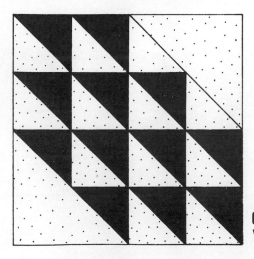

Ocean Waves
Variation 3

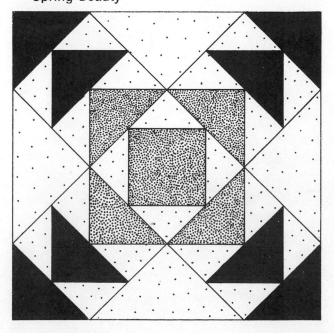

Old Maid's Ramble
Variation 4
  Lady of the Lake, Var. 3

Path Through the Woods

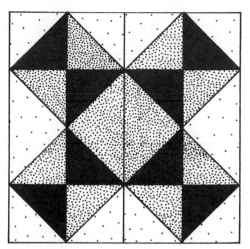

Old Tippecanoe

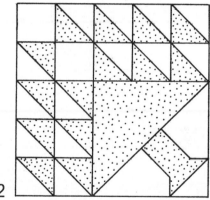

Pine Tree
Variation 2

Palm Leaves Hosannah!
  Hosanna
  Palm
  Palm Leaf, Var. 1

Pine Tree   Variation 3
  Temperance Tree, Var. 2

43

Pine Tree
Variation 4

Ribbon Border

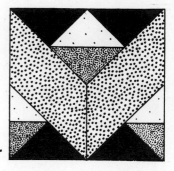

Pinwheel Star

Ribbons

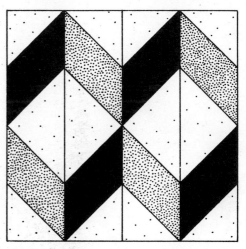

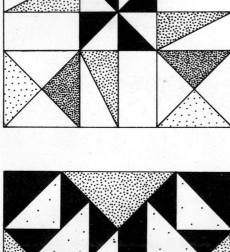

Railroad Crossing
Variation 1

Rolling Pinwheel
Variation 1

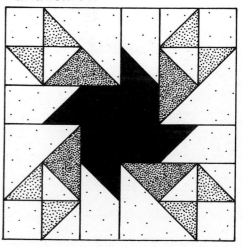

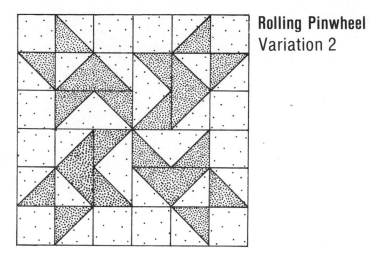

**Rolling Pinwheel
Variation 2**

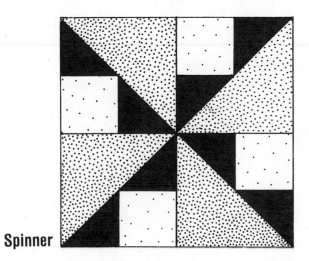

Sailboats

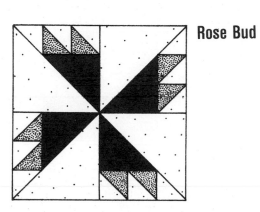

Rose Bud

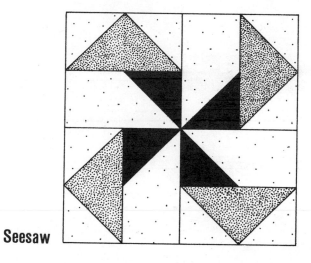

Seesaw

Sailboat

Spinner

45

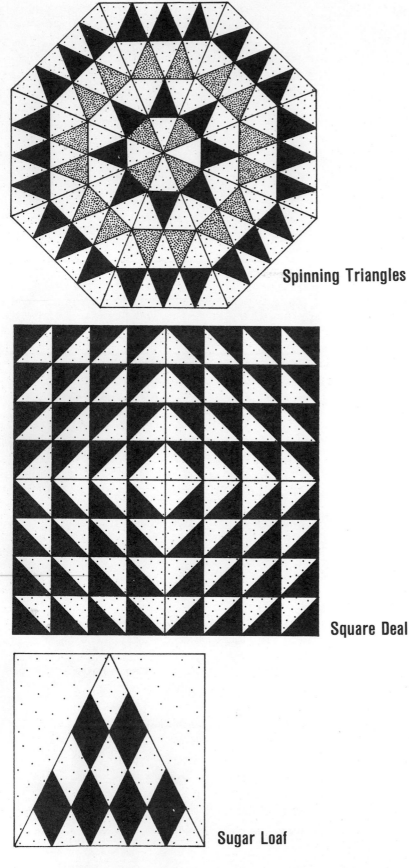

Spinning Triangles

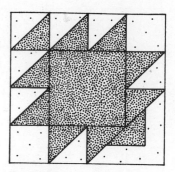

Swallow

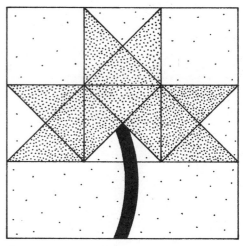

Sweet Gum Leaf

Square Deal

Sugar Loaf

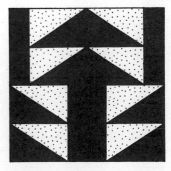

Tall Pine Tree

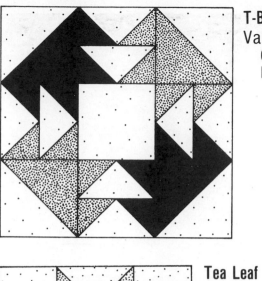

T-Blocks
Variation 1
   Capital T
   Double-T, Var. 2

Thousand Pyramids
   Pyramids
   Triangles

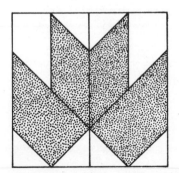

Tea Leaf
Variation 1

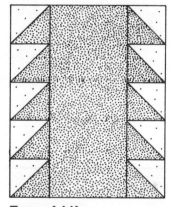

Tree of Life
Variation 2

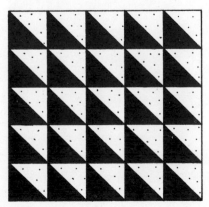

Tea Leaf
Variation 2

Tents of Armageddon

Tree of Paradise
Variation 1

Tree of Paradise
Variation 2

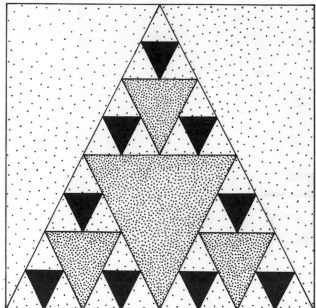

Triangular Triangles

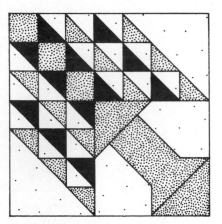

Tree of Paradise
Variation 3

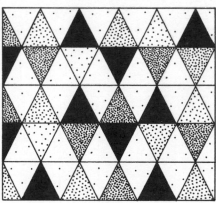

Tumblers
Variation 1

Triangle Puzzle

Twenty-four Triangles

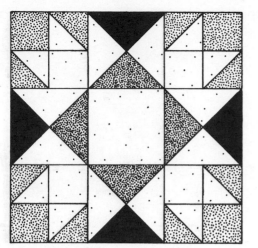

Union Squares

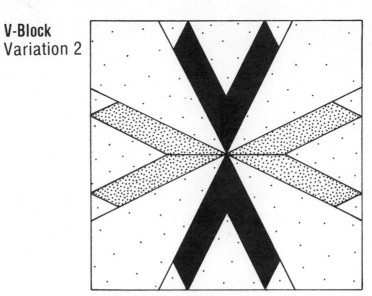

V-Block
Variation 2

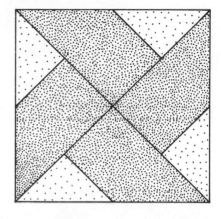

Water Wheel
Variation 2
Whirlwind

Unknown Four-Patch

Whirligig
Variation 2

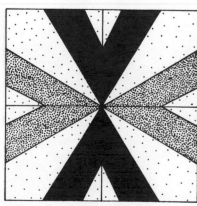

V-Block   Variation 1

Wild Goose Chase
Variation 1

Windmill Variation 1
Crow's Foot, Var. 3
Fan Mill, Var. 1
Flutter Wheels, Var. 1
Fly, Var. 1
Honey's Choice
Kathy's Ramble, Var. 1
Mill Wheel, Var. 1
Old Windmill
Pinwheel, Var. 1
Slash Diagonal
Sugar Bowl, Var. 1
Water Mill
Water Wheel, Var. 1

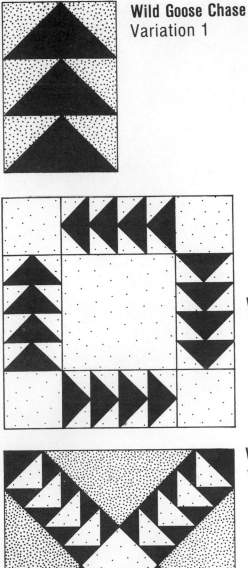

Wild Goose Chase
Variation 4

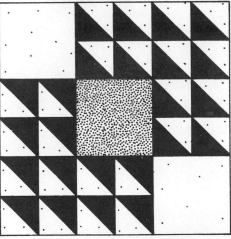

Windmill
Variation 4

Wild Goose Chase
Variation 5

Winged Square
Variation 1
Cut Glass Dish
Golden Gates

Windblown Square
Balkan Puzzle
Zigzag Tile

Yankee Puzzle
Variation 1
Hourglass, Var. 2

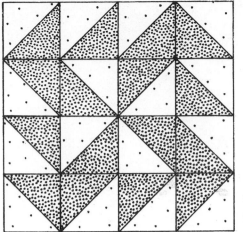

Yankee Puzzle
Variation 2

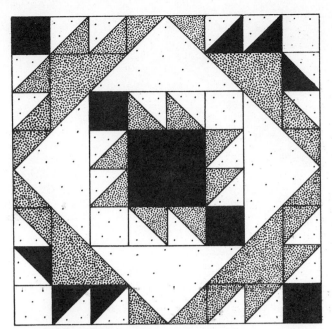

Indian Hatchet

SUPPLEMENT

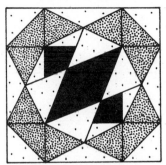

Dove in the Window Variation 2

Rocky Glen
Variation 4
Lost Ships

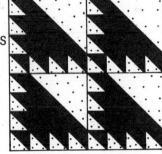

**Free Trade
Block**

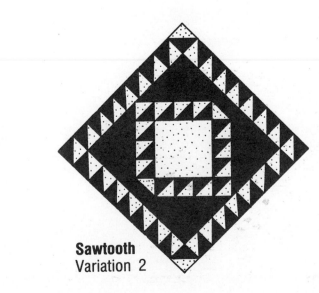

Sawtooth
Variation 2

51

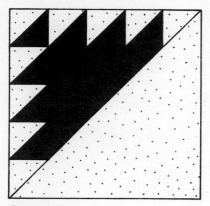

Sawtooth
Variation 4

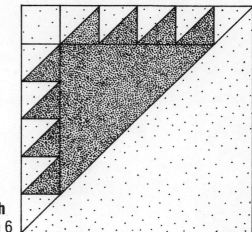

Sawtooth
Variation 6

Circles

Around the World

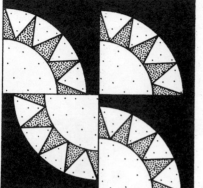

Baby Bunting

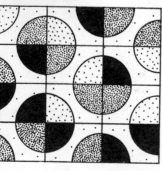

Baseball

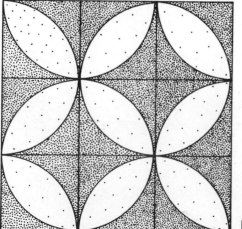

Bay Leaf

Buttercup
Robbing Peter to
  Pay Paul, Var. 6
Wheel of Mystery
Winding Ways

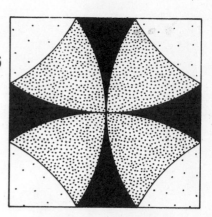

Circle Cross

Circular Saw
  Four Little Fans
  Oriole Window

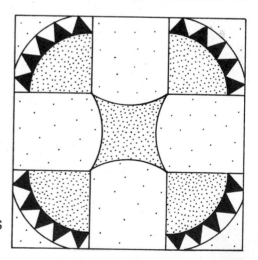

Clamshell

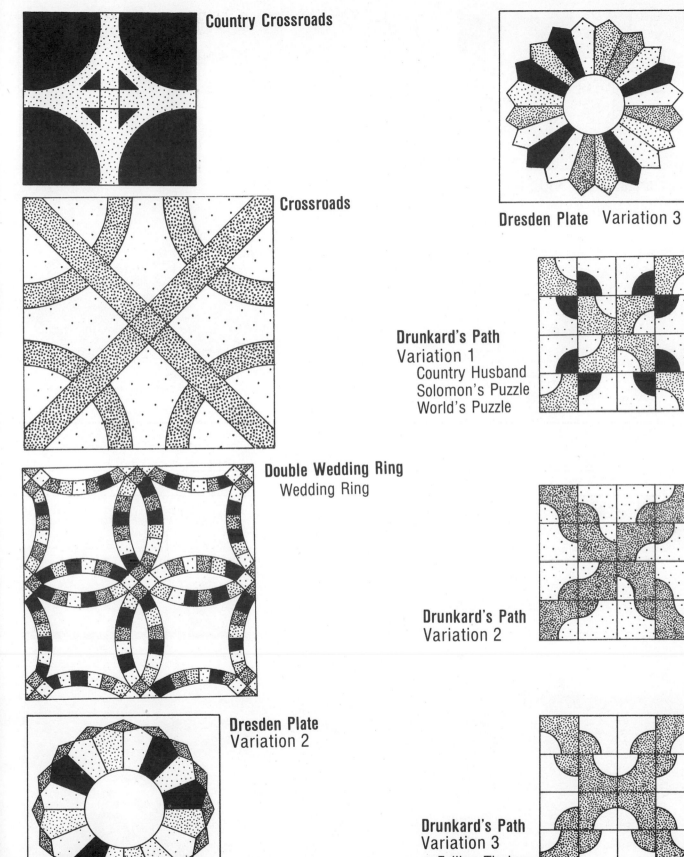

Country Crossroads

Crossroads

Dresden Plate Variation 3

Drunkard's Path
Variation 1
    Country Husband
    Solomon's Puzzle
    World's Puzzle

Double Wedding Ring
Wedding Ring

Drunkard's Path
Variation 2

Dresden Plate
Variation 2

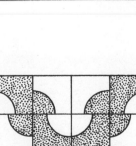

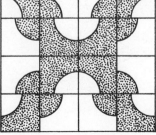

Drunkard's Path
Variation 3
    Falling Timber

55

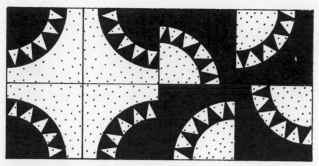

Drunkard's Path   Variation 4

Friendship Ring
Aster
Dresden Plate,
Var. 1

Flo's Fan

Full-blown Tulip
Variation 2

Fool's Puzzle
Variation 1

Grandmother's Fan
Fan
Fanny's Fan, Var. 1

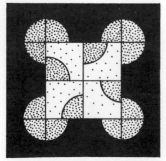

Fool's Puzzle
Variation 2

Hearts and Gizzards
Lazy Daisy, Var. 1
Petal Quilt
Pierrot's Pom-pon
Springtime Blossom
Wheel of Fortune, Var. 1
Windmill, Var. 2

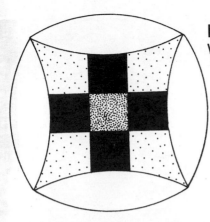

Improved Nine-patch
Variation 1
    Bailey Nine-Patch
    Glorified Nine-Patch

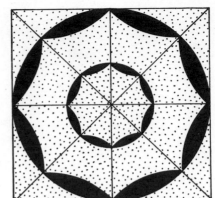

Odds and Ends

Lafayette Orange Peel
    Melon Patch
    Orange Peel, Var. 2

Love Ring
    Lone Ring
    Nonesuch

Orange Peel
Variation 1
    Compass, Var. 1
    Dolly Madison's Workbox, Var. 2
    Robbing Peter to Pay Paul, Var. 4

Missouri Beauty

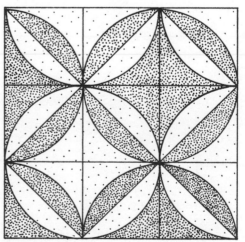

Orange Peel
Variation 3
    Dolly Madison's Workbox, Var. 1
    Rob Peter to Pay Paul, Var. 2

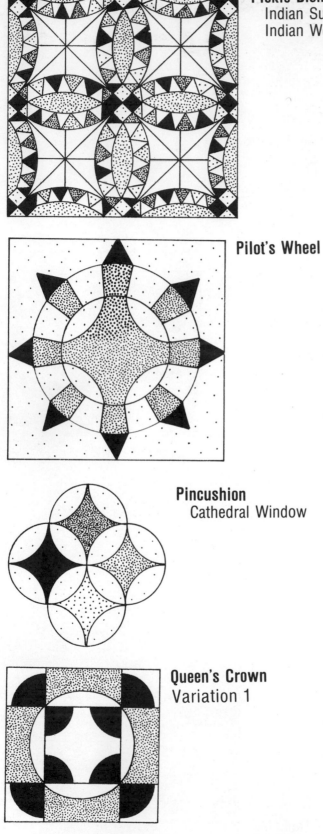

Pickle Dish
Indian Summer
Indian Wedding Ring

Pilot's Wheel

Pincushion
Cathedral Window

Queen's Crown
Variation 1

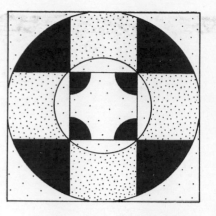

Queen's Crown
Variation 2

Queen's Pride

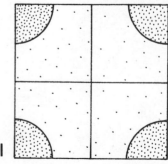

Rebecca's Fan

Reverse Baseball

Robbing Peter to Pay Paul
Variation 2

Signature

Robbing Peter to Pay Paul

Variation 3
    Falling Timbers
    Vine of Friendship

Snowball Variation 1
    Mill Wheel, Var. 2
    Old Mill Wheel
    Pullman Puzzle

Rob Peter to Pay Paul
Variation 1

Snowball Variation 2
    Compass, Var. 3

Rocky Road to Dublin

Snowball
Variation 4

59

Snowball Wreath

Steeplechase
Bows and Arrows

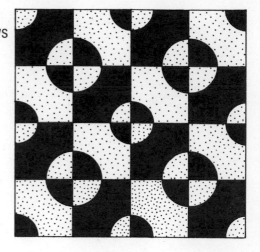

Strawberry
Full-Blown Tulip, Var. 1
Oriental Star, Var. 2

Spools
Always Friends
Friendship Chain

Turkey Tracks
Variation 1
Wandering Foot

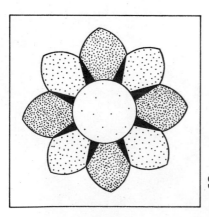

Star Flower Variation 1
Golden Glow, Var. 1

Unnamed
Variation 1

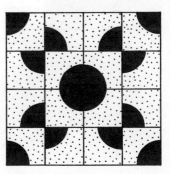

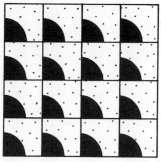

Unnamed   Variation 2

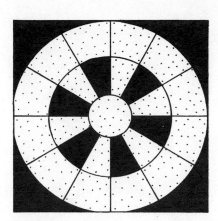

Wheel of Fortune   Variation 4

Victoria's Crown

Wheel of Fortune   Variation 5

Wheel of Chance
True Lover's Buggy Wheel

Wonder of the World

SUPPLEMENT

Reel

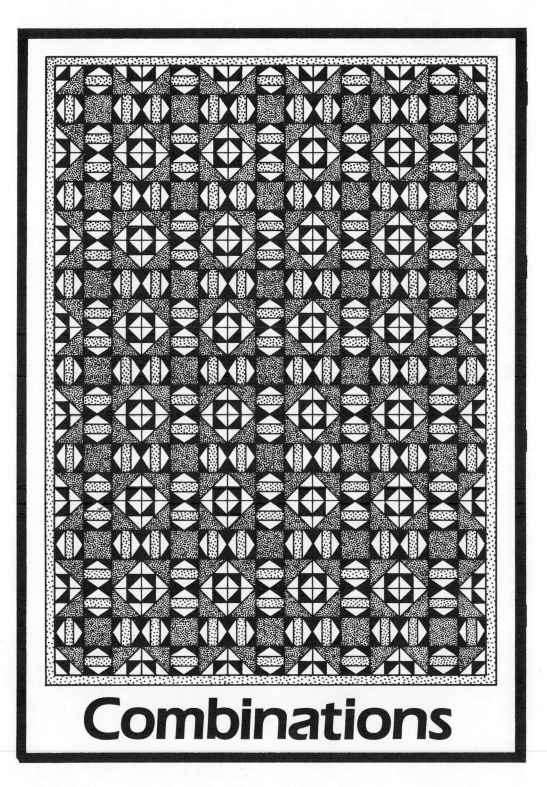

Combinations

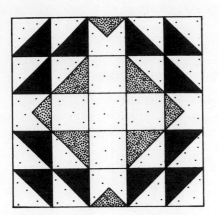

Album Variation 1

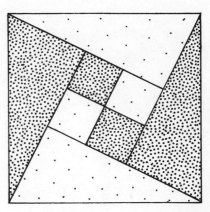

Arabic Lattice

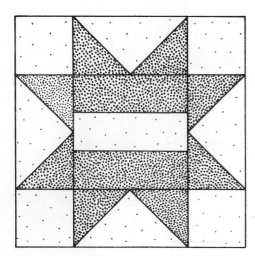

Album Variation 2

Arrowheads Variation 1

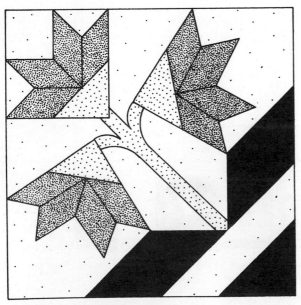

Antique Shop Tulip
Double Tulip

Aunt Sukey's Choice
Puss 'n' Boots

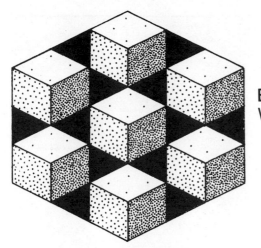

Baby Blocks
Variation 2

Baskets

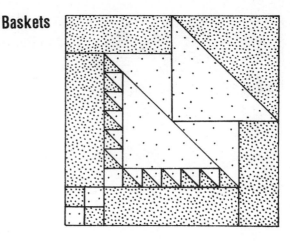

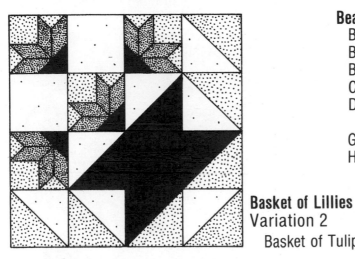

Bear Tracks Variation 1
   Bear's Foot
   Bear's Paw, Var. 3
   Bear's Track, Var. 1
   Cross and Crown, Var. 3
   Duck's Foot in the Mud,
      Var. 2
   Goose Tracks, Var. 1
   Hand of Friendship, Var. 2

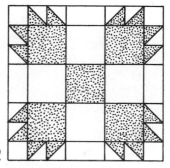

Illinois Turkey Track
Lily Design

Basket of Lillies
Variation 2
   Basket of Tulips, Var. 2

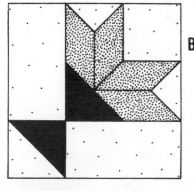

Basket of Scraps
   Cactus Basket, Var. 2
   Desert Rose, Var. 2
   Texas Rose, Var. 2
   Texas Treasure, Var. 2

Bear Tracks
Variation 2
   Bear's Track, Var. 2

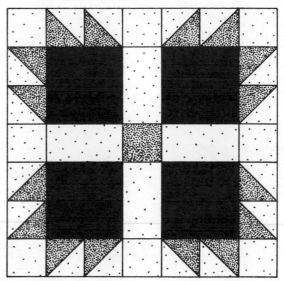

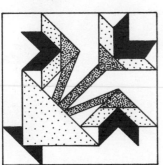

Basket of Tulips
Variation 1
   Basket of Lilies, Var. 1

Beggar's Block
Cats and Mice, Var. 2

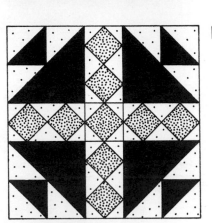

Bird's Nest

Blackford's Beauty

Blocks and Stars

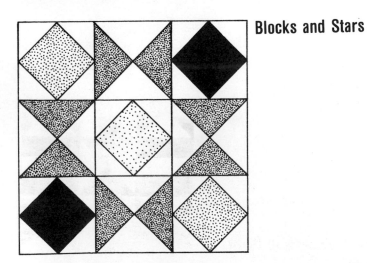

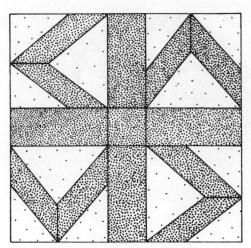

Bow Knot
Farmer's Puzzle
Swastika, Var. 1

Boxed Ts

Braced Star

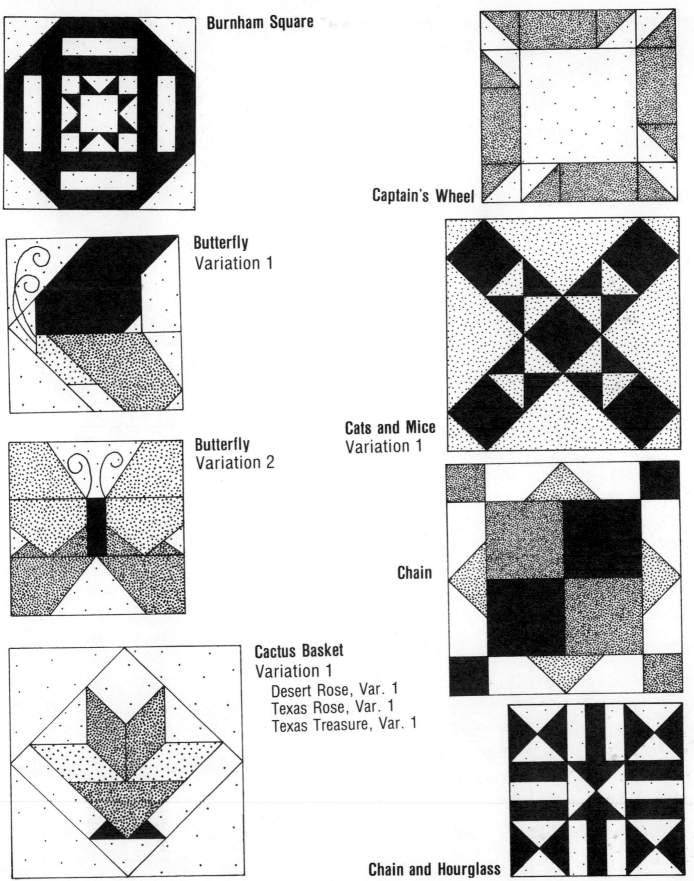

Burnham Square

Butterfly
Variation 1

Butterfly
Variation 2

Cactus Basket
Variation 1
    Desert Rose, Var. 1
    Texas Rose, Var. 1
    Texas Treasure, Var. 1

Captain's Wheel

Cats and Mice
Variation 1

Chain

Chain and Hourglass

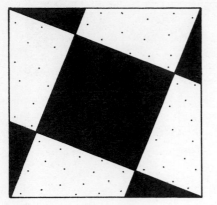

Checkerboard Skew

Christmas Star
Variation 2

Children of Israel

Churn Dash Variation 1
Lover's Knot
Monkey Wrench, Var. 1

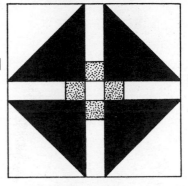

Churn Dash
Variation 2

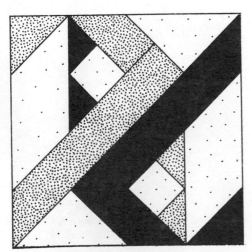

Chinese Puzzle Variation 1

Claws

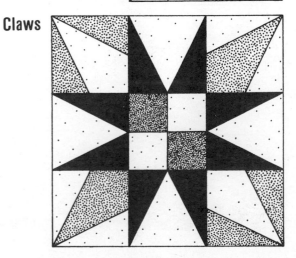

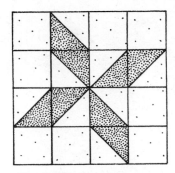

Clay's Choice
Harry's Star
Henry of the West
Jackson's Star, Var. 2
Star of the West, Var. 3

Crazy Ann   Variation 2

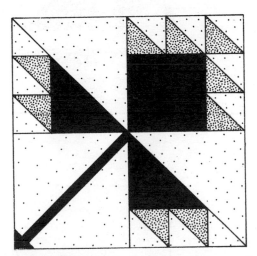

Clover Blossom
English Ivy

Crazy House

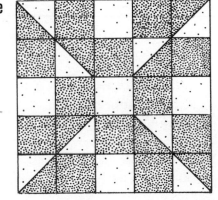

Combination Star
Ornate Star

Cross and Crown
Variation 1

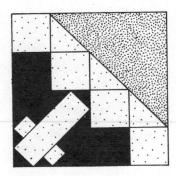

69

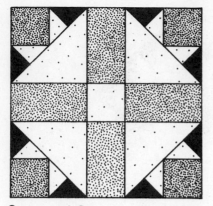

Cross and Crown Variation 4

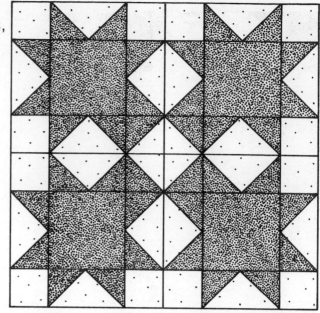

Crow Foot
Devil's Claws,
Var. 2

Cross Upon a Cross

Cross and Crown, Var. 2
Crown and Cross
Crowned Cross, Var. 1
Golgotha, Var. 2
Three Crosses, Var. 2

Crown and Thorns
Crown of Thorns
Georgetown Circle, Var. 1
Memory Wreath, Var. 1
Single Wedding Ring,
Var. 1

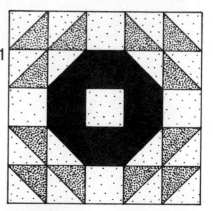

Crow's Foot
Variation 4

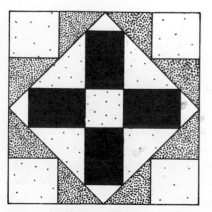

Cross Within a Cross

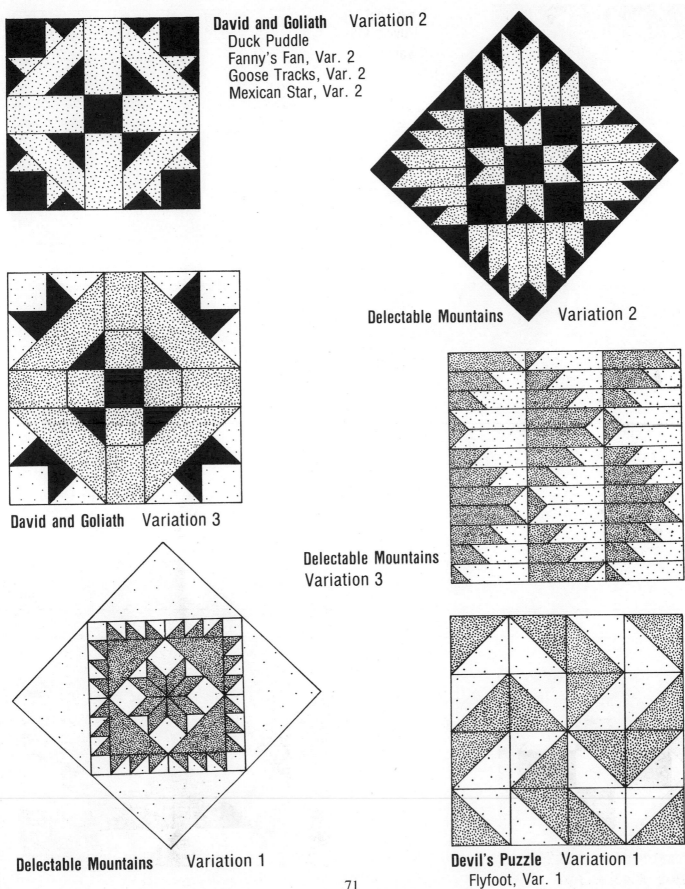

David and Goliath Variation 2
Duck Puddle
Fanny's Fan, Var. 2
Goose Tracks, Var. 2
Mexican Star, Var. 2

Delectable Mountains Variation 2

David and Goliath Variation 3

Delectable Mountains
Variation 3

Delectable Mountains Variation 1

Devil's Puzzle Variation 1
Flyfoot, Var. 1

71

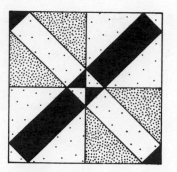

Devil's Puzzle   Variation 2
Flyfoot, Var. 2

Double Square
Variation 1

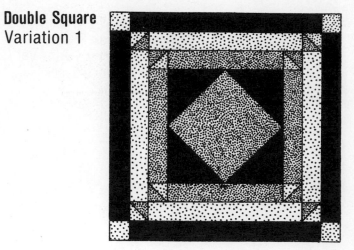

Dogwood Blossoms

Double X   Variation 1

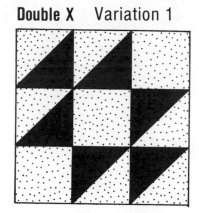

Domino and Squares

Dove in the Window   Variation 2

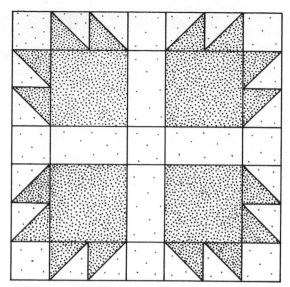

Duck's Foot

Dutch Mill

Duck's Foot in the Mud
Variation 1
   Bear's Paw, Var. 1
   Crow's Foot, Var. 1
   Hand of Friendship, Var. 1

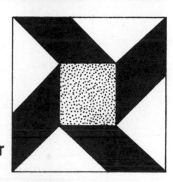

Eccentric Star
Variation 1

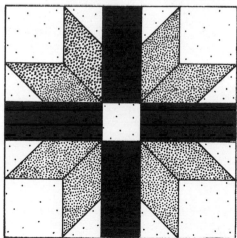

E-Z Quilt

Dusty Miller

Fannie's Fan
Variation 1

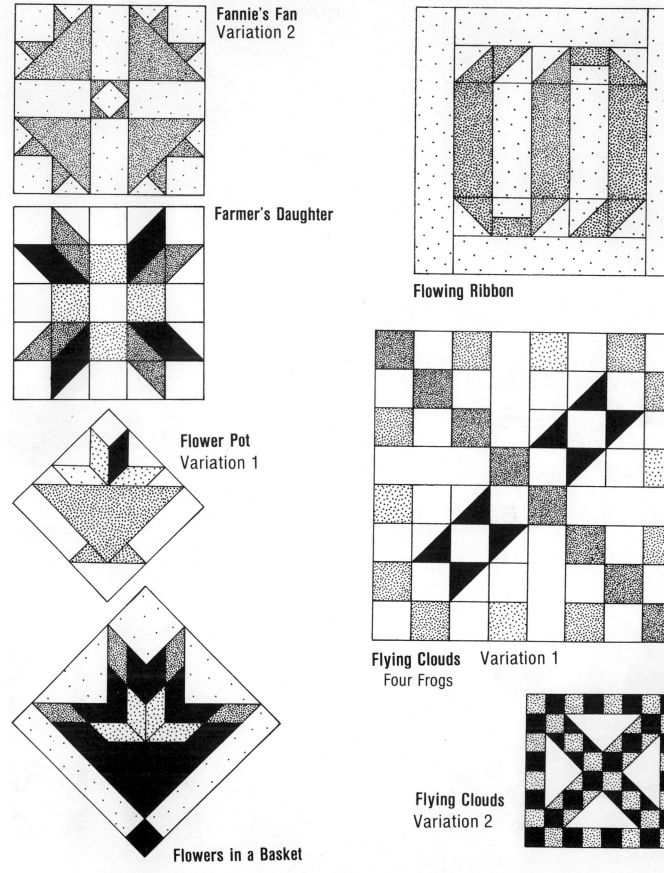

Fannie's Fan
Variation 2

Farmer's Daughter

Flower Pot
Variation 1

Flowing Ribbon

Flying Clouds Variation 1
Four Frogs

Flying Clouds
Variation 2

Flowers in a Basket

74

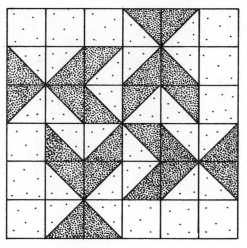

Flying Dutchman   Variation 1

Four Little Baskets

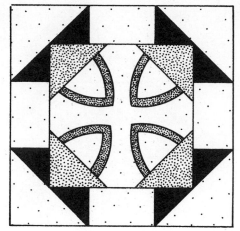

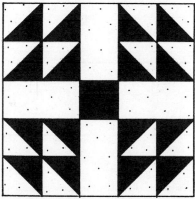

Flying Geese   Variation 2
Handy Andy, Var. 6

Friendship Knot

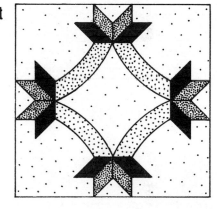

Four Darts
   Bull's Eye
   David and Goliath, Var. 1
   Doe and Darts
   Flying Darts

Garden of Eden   Variation 1

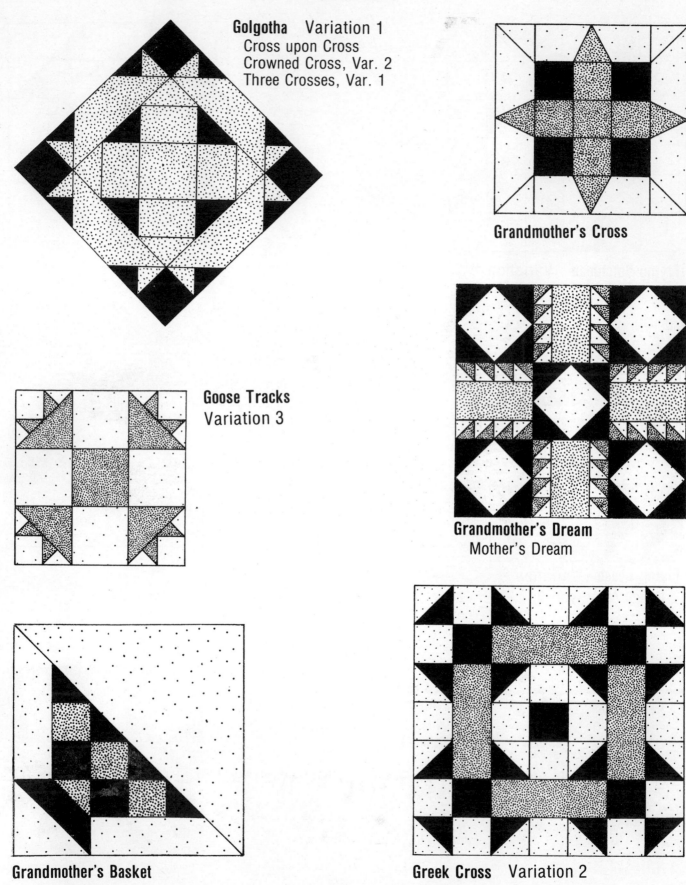

Golgotha Variation 1
Cross upon Cross
Crowned Cross, Var. 2
Three Crosses, Var. 1

Grandmother's Cross

Goose Tracks
Variation 3

Grandmother's Dream
Mother's Dream

Grandmother's Basket

Greek Cross Variation 2

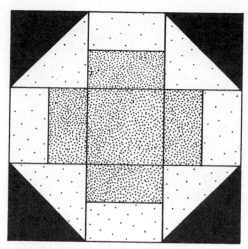

Greek Cross   Variation 3
Grecian
Grecian Design

Hayes' Corner

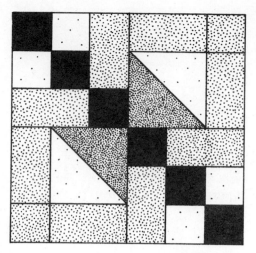

Heart's Desire

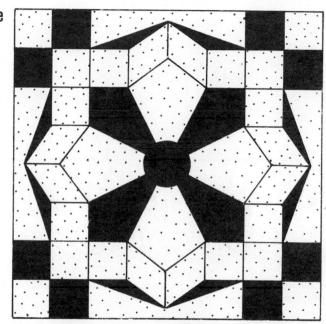

Handy Andy   Variation 2

Hen and Chickens
Variation 2

Handy Andy   Variation 3

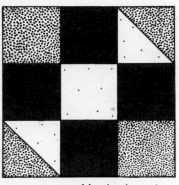

Hourglass Variation 1

Indian Hatchet
Variation 2

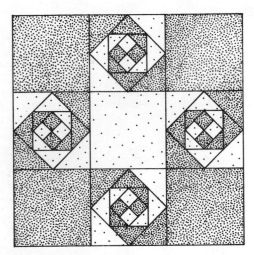

Indiana Puzzle
  Monkey Wrench, Var. 3

Indian Meadows Variation 1
  Mountain Meadows
  Queen Charlotte's Crown,
    Var. 1

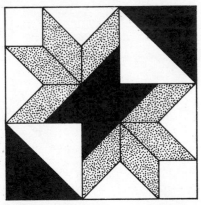

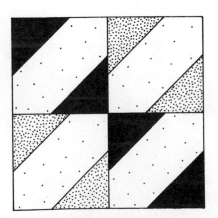

Indian Hatchet Variation 1

Irish Chain
Variation 1

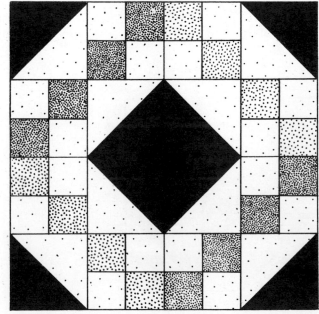

Jack in the Box
  Whirligig, Var. 1

Joseph's Coat   Variation 1
  Scrap-Bag

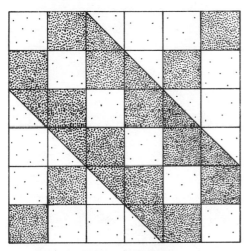

Jacob's Ladder   Variation 1

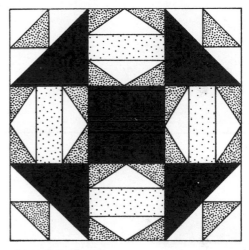

Joseph's Coat
  Mollie's Choice   Variation 2

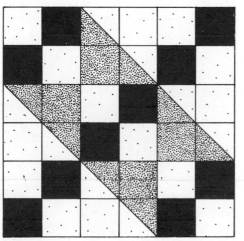

Jacob's Ladder   Variation 2
  Road to California, Var. 1
  Rocky Road to California
  Stepping Stones, Var. 1
  Tail of Benjamin's Kite
  Trail of the Covered Wagon
  Underground Railroad
  Wagon Tracks

King David's Crown   Variation 2

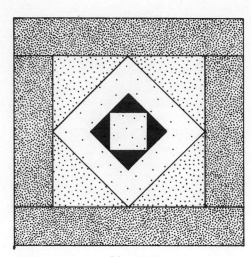

King's Crown Variation 1

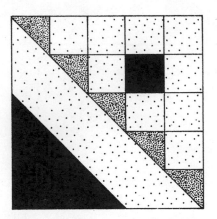

King's Crown Variation 2
Greek Cross, Var. 1

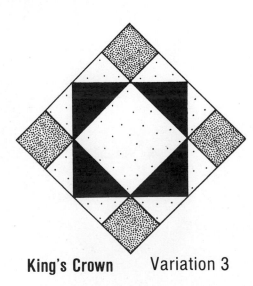

King's Crown Variation 3

Ladies' Delight

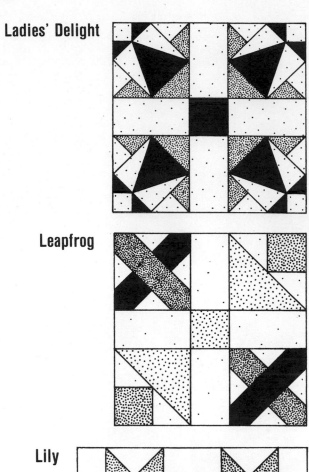

Leapfrog

Lily

Lily of the Field

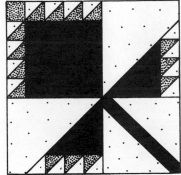

Little Giant

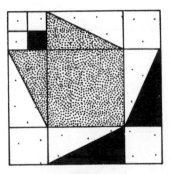

Magnolia Bud

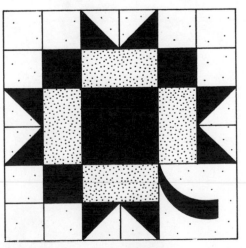

Maple Leaf   Variation 1

Maple Leaf
Variation 2
　Palm Leaf, Var. 2
　Poplar Leaf

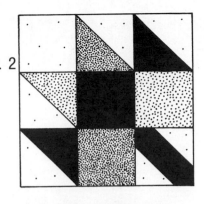

Mare's Nest

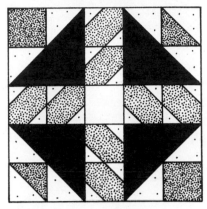

Mary Tenney Gray Travel Club Patch

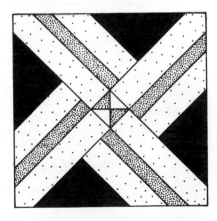

Memory Block

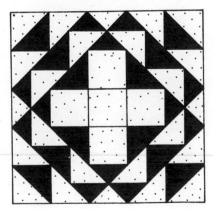

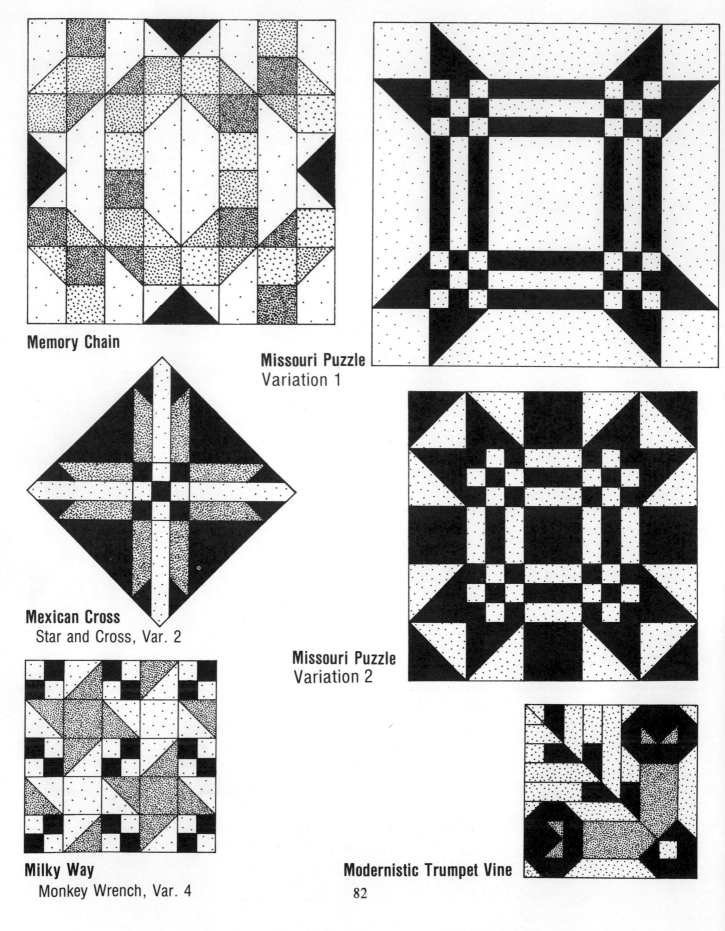

Memory Chain

Missouri Puzzle
Variation 1

Mexican Cross
Star and Cross, Var. 2

Missouri Puzzle
Variation 2

Milky Way
Monkey Wrench, Var. 4

Modernistic Trumpet Vine

Mother's Fancy Star

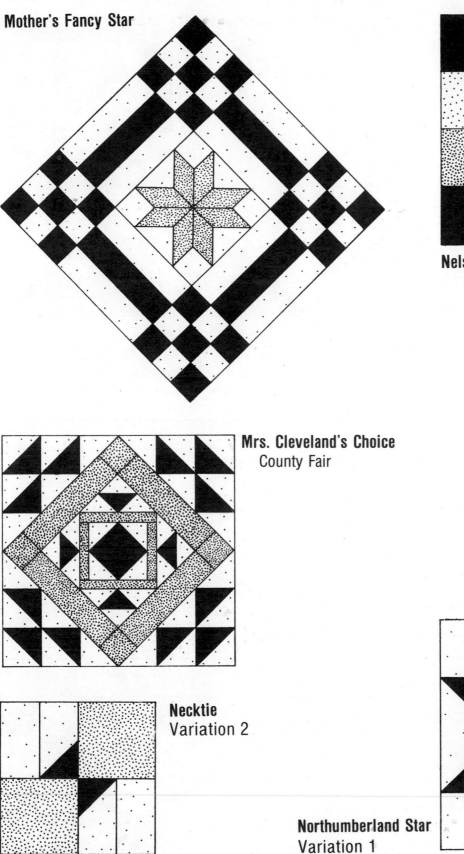

Nelson's Victory

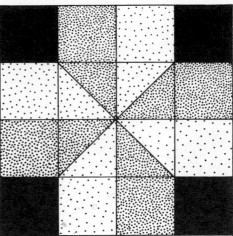

Mrs. Cleveland's Choice
County Fair

Nine-patch Variation 2

Necktie
Variation 2

Northumberland Star
Variation 1

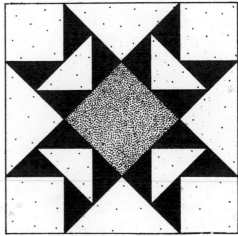

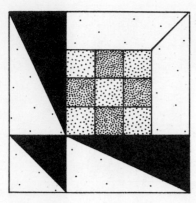

Nosegay Variation 2

Philadelphia Pavement

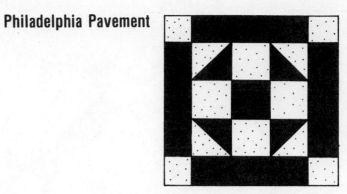

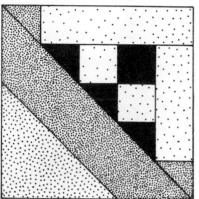

Old King Cole's Crown

Pieced Pyramids

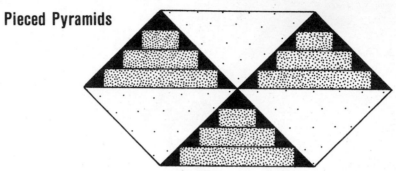

Pieced Star Variation 2
Octagonal Star, Var. 2

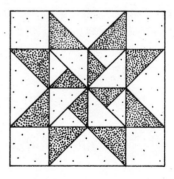

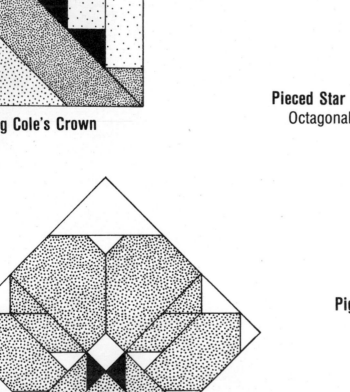

Pansy

Pigeon Toes

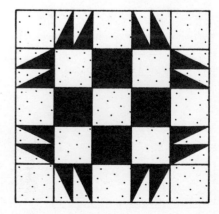

Pine Burr

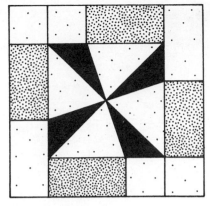

Pinwheel Skew

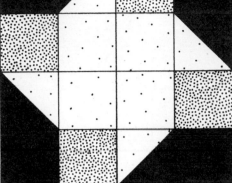

Pinwheel Variation 2
Crow's Foot, Var. 2
Fan Mill, Var. 2
Flutter Wheels, Var. 2
Fly, Var. 2
Foot
Kathy's Ramble, Var. 2
Sugar Bowl, Var. 2

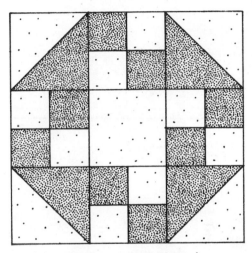

Prairie Queen Variation 1

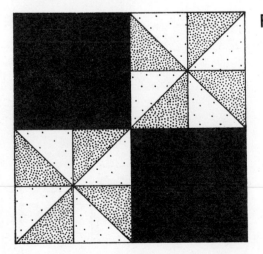

Pinwheels

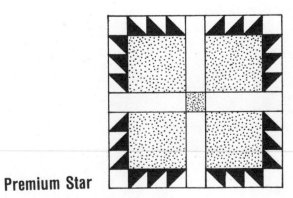

Premium Star

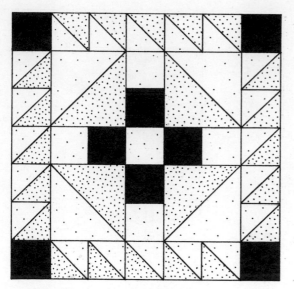

Prickly Pear Variation 1

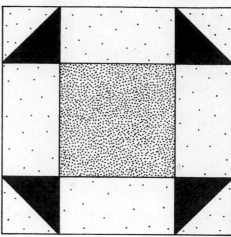

Puss in the Corner
Variation 1
    Kitty Corner, Var. 2
    Tic Tac Toe, Var. 2

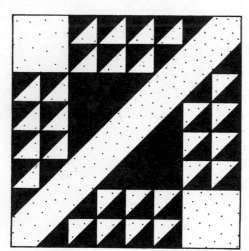

Primrose Path

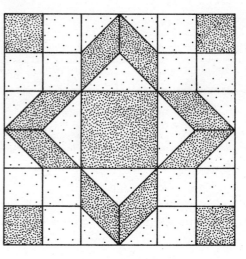

Puss in the Corner
Variation 2
    Puss in Boots

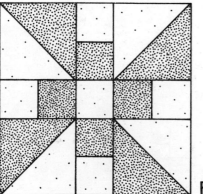

Propellor

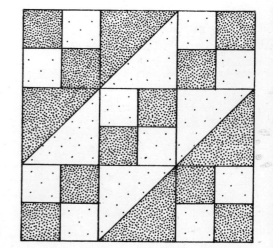

Railroad

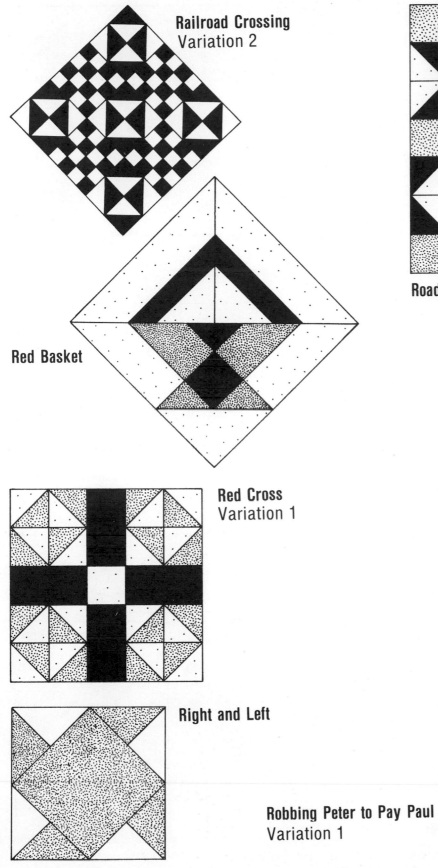

Railroad Crossing
Variation 2

Red Basket

Red Cross
Variation 1

Right and Left

Road to California   **Variation 3**

Road to California   **Variation 4**

Robbing Peter to Pay Paul
Variation 1

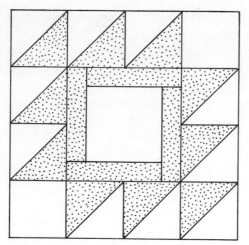

Rocky Mountain Puzzle

Sawtooth
Variation 3

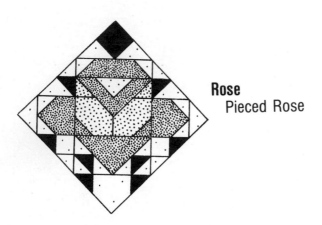

Rose
Pieced Rose

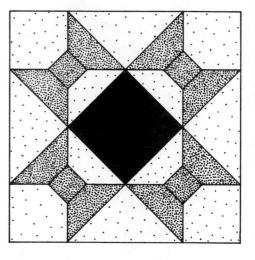

Secret Drawer

Shadows

Royal Cross

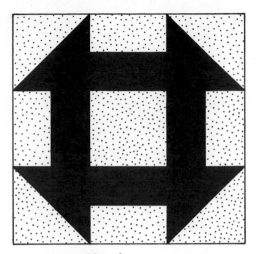

Sister's Choice
Four-X Star
Five-Patch Star

Sherman's March

Barn Door	Love Knot
Double Monkey Wrench	Monkey Wrench, Var. 2
Hole in the Barn Door	Quail's Nest
Lincoln's Platform	

Square and a Half

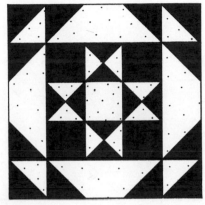

Square Within Squares

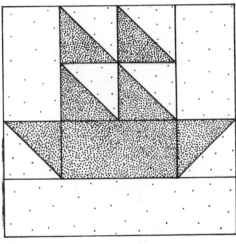

Ship

Shoofly Variation 1
Chinese Coin
Grandmother's Choice, Var. 2
Star Spangled Banner

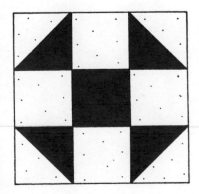

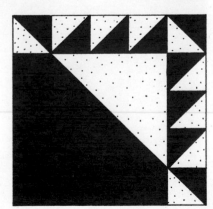

Star of Hope
Variation 1

Starry Lane

Swing in the Center

Stepping Stones

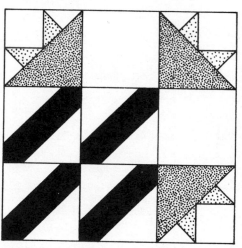

Storm at Sea   Variation 2
Rolling Stone, Var. 1

Tassal Point

T-Blocks   Variation 2

Suspension Bridge

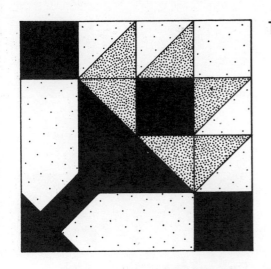

Tea Basket

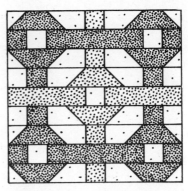

Tile Puzzle Variation 2

Toad in the Puddle Variation 1

Thelma's Choice

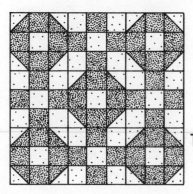

Toad in the Puddle
Variation 2
    Double Square, Var. 2
    Jack in the Pulpit

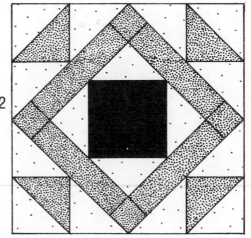

Tile Puzzle Variation 1
Improved Nine-Patch, Var. 2
Puzzled Tile

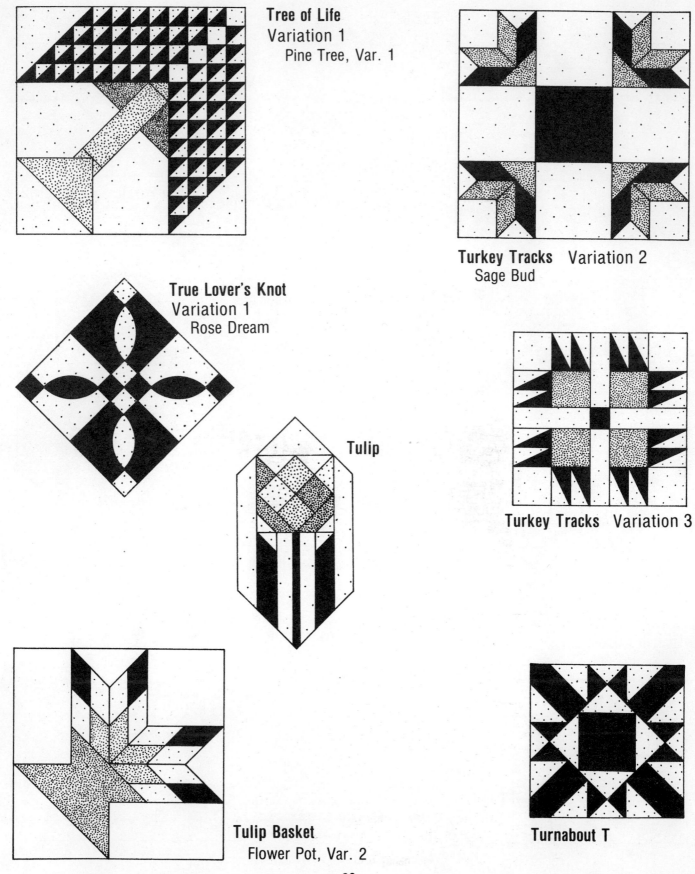

Tree of Life
Variation 1
Pine Tree, Var. 1

Turkey Tracks Variation 2
Sage Bud

True Lover's Knot
Variation 1
Rose Dream

Tulip

Turkey Tracks Variation 3

Tulip Basket
Flower Pot, Var. 2

Turnabout T

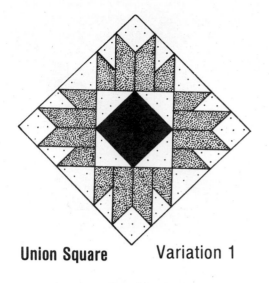

Union Square   Variation 1

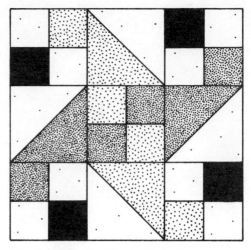

Water Wheel   Variation 3

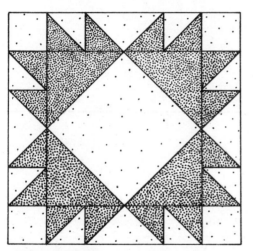

Union Square   Variation 2

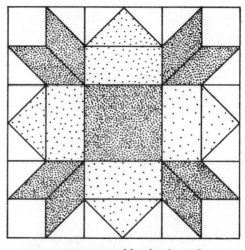

Weather Vane   Variation 2

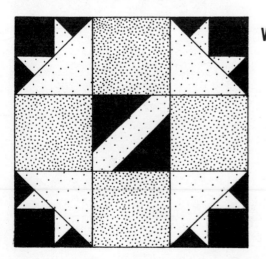

W.C.T.U.

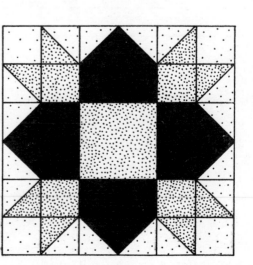

Weather Vane
Variation 3

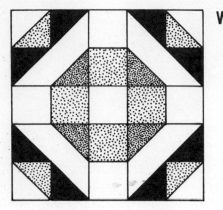

Wedding Rings

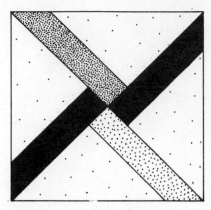

Windmill Variation 3

White Cross

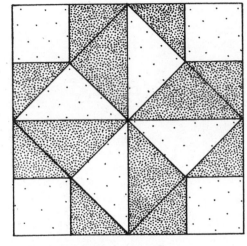

Windmill Variation 5

Wild Goose Chase Variation 3

Wishing Ring

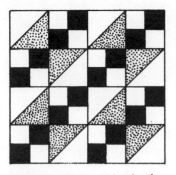

World's Fair Variation 1

X-Quartet

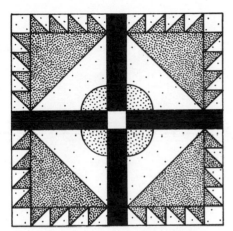

World's Fair Variation 2

X-Quisite

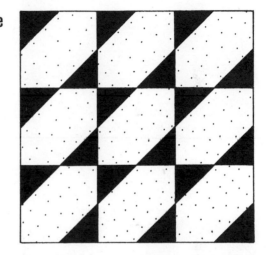

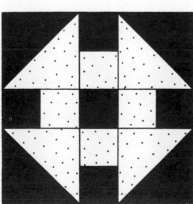

Wrench

Young Man's Fancy
Goose in the Pond, Var. 2
Mrs. Wolf's Red Beauty

95

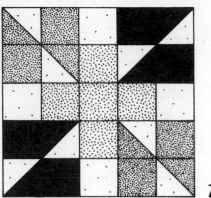

Z-Cross

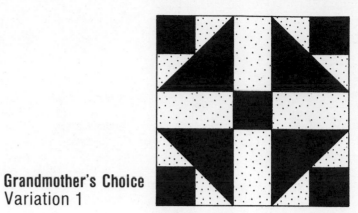

Grandmother's Choice
Variation 1

SUPPLEMENT

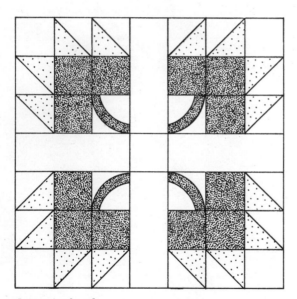

Autumn Leaf

Nosegay

St. George's Cross

54-40 or Fight

Squares

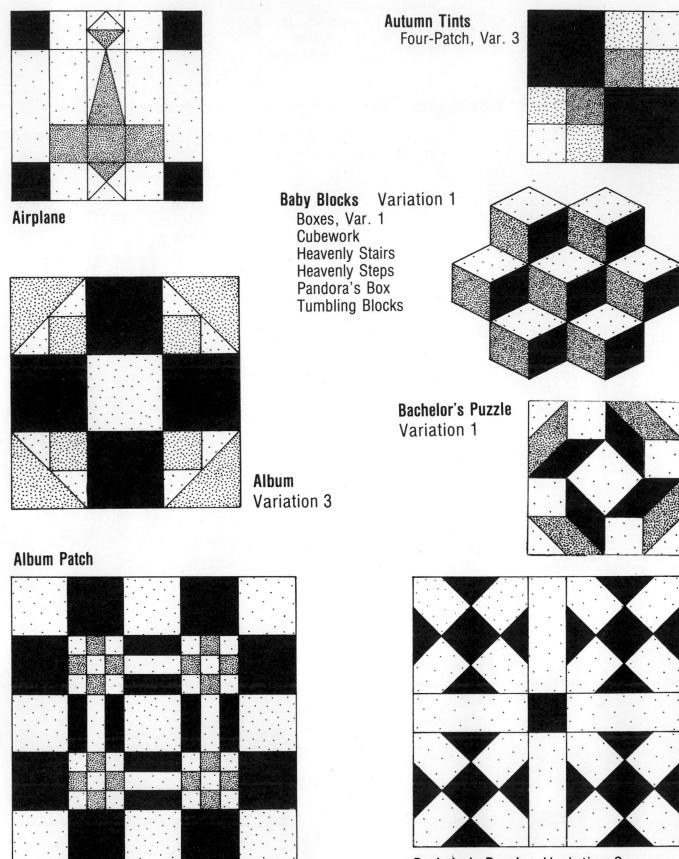

Airplane

Autumn Tints
Four-Patch, Var. 3

Baby Blocks   Variation 1
 Boxes, Var. 1
 Cubework
 Heavenly Stairs
 Heavenly Steps
 Pandora's Box
 Tumbling Blocks

Album
Variation 3

Bachelor's Puzzle
Variation 1

Album Patch

Bachelor's Puzzle   Variation 2

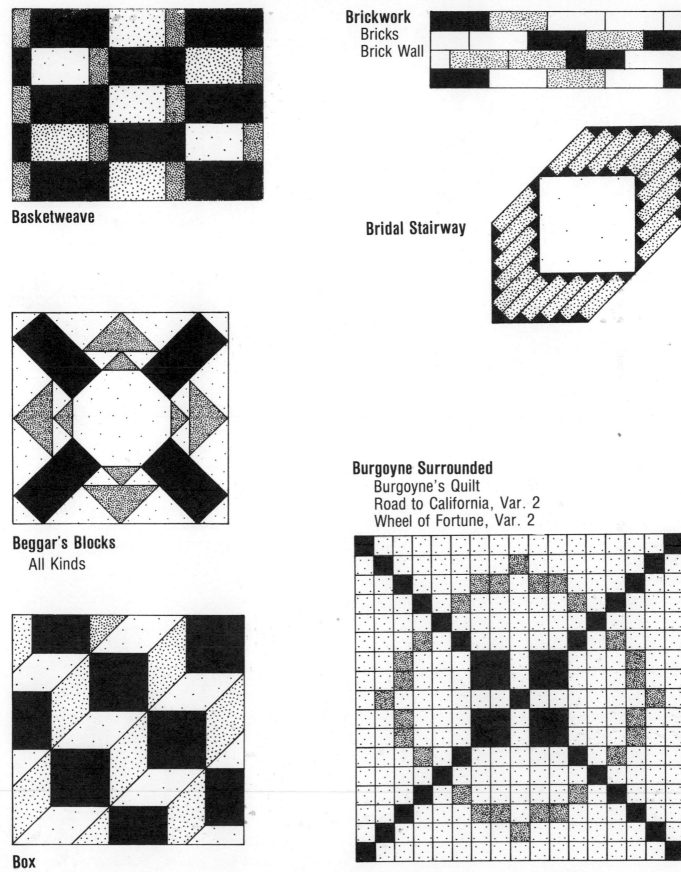

Basketweave

Brickwork
Bricks
Brick Wall

Bridal Stairway

Beggar's Blocks
All Kinds

Burgoyne Surrounded
Burgoyne's Quilt
Road to California, Var. 2
Wheel of Fortune, Var. 2

Box

99

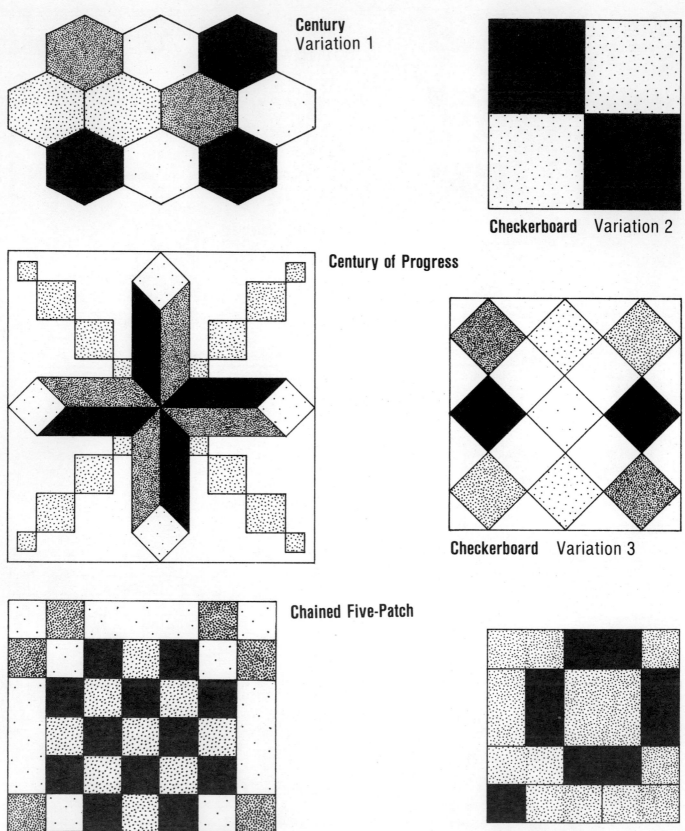

Century
Variation 1

Checkerboard Variation 2

Century of Progress

Checkerboard Variation 3

Chained Five-Patch

Children's Delight

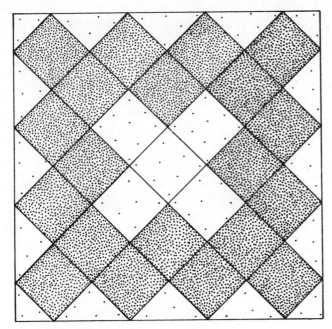

Christian Cross

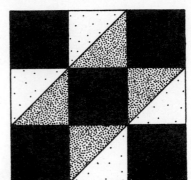

Contrary Wife

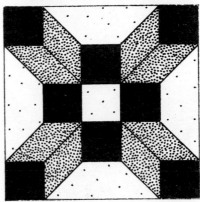

Corner Posts

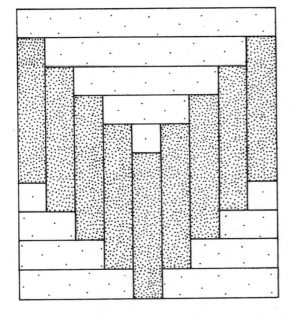

Coarsewoven
Variation 2
Finewoven, Var. 2

Country Roads

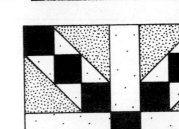

Coffin Star
Picket Fence

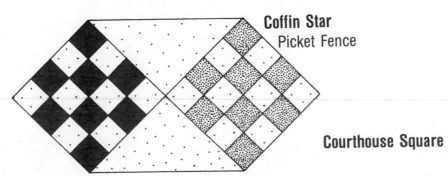

Courthouse Square

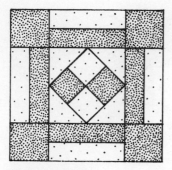

Coxey's Camp

Domino Variation 1

Cross Variation 2

Domino Variation 2

Domino and Square

Cupid's Arrowpoint

Double Irish Chain
Double Irish Cross

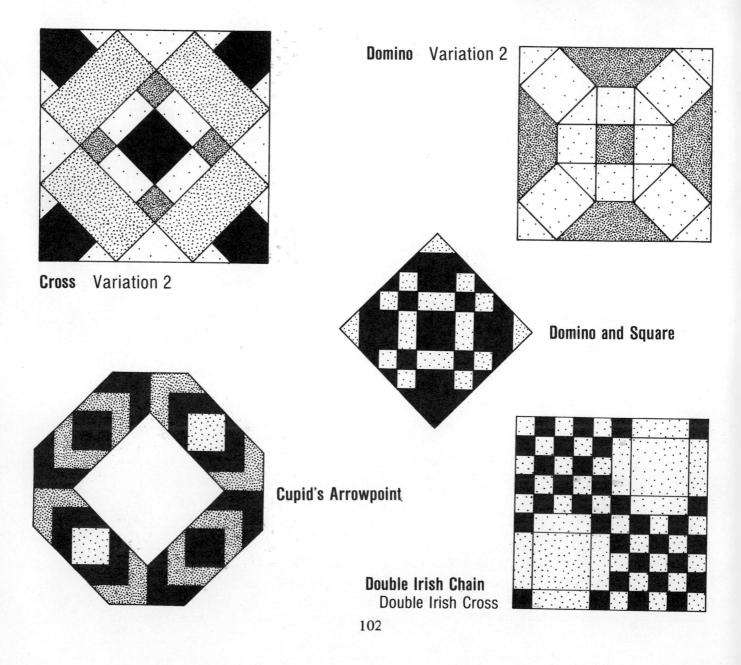

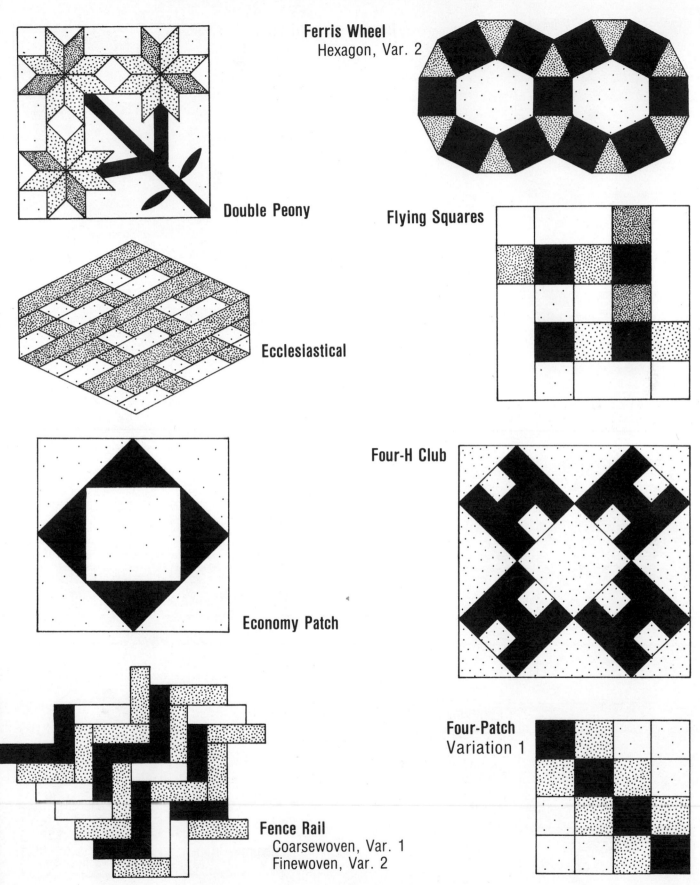

Ferris Wheel
Hexagon, Var. 2

Double Peony

Ecclesiastical

Flying Squares

Four-H Club

Economy Patch

Fence Rail
Coarsewoven, Var. 1
Finewoven, Var. 2

Four-Patch
Variation 1

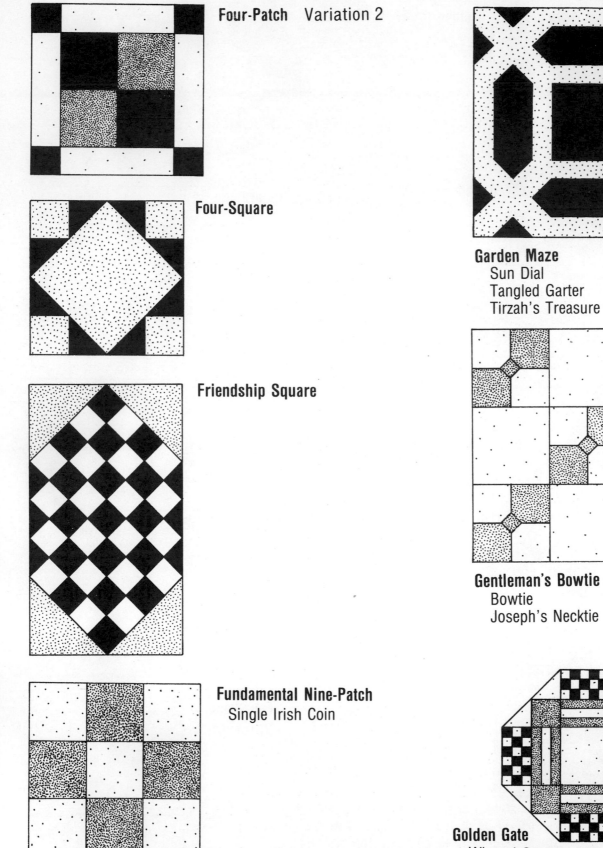

Four-Patch Variation 2

Four-Square

Friendship Square

Fundamental Nine-Patch
Single Irish Coin

Garden Maze
Sun Dial
Tangled Garter
Tirzah's Treasure

Gentleman's Bowtie
Bowtie
Joseph's Necktie

Golden Gate
Winged Square, Var. 2

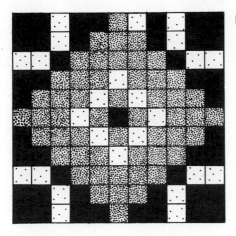

Golden Glow Variation 2

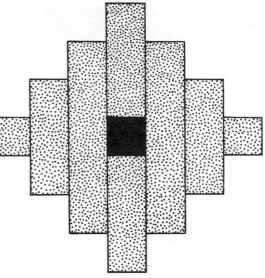

Granny's Flower Garden

Grandma's Red and White

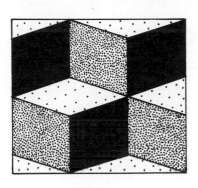

Grandmother's Flower Garden
    Flower Garden   Rainbow Tile
    French Bouquet   Rosette
    Grandma's Garden   Spider Web, Var. 1
    Honeycomb, Var. 1
    Job's Troubles, Var. 1
    Martha Washington's Flower Garden
    Mosaic

Hand
    California Oakleaf   True Lover's Knot, Var. 2
    Sassafras Leaf

Hanging Diamond

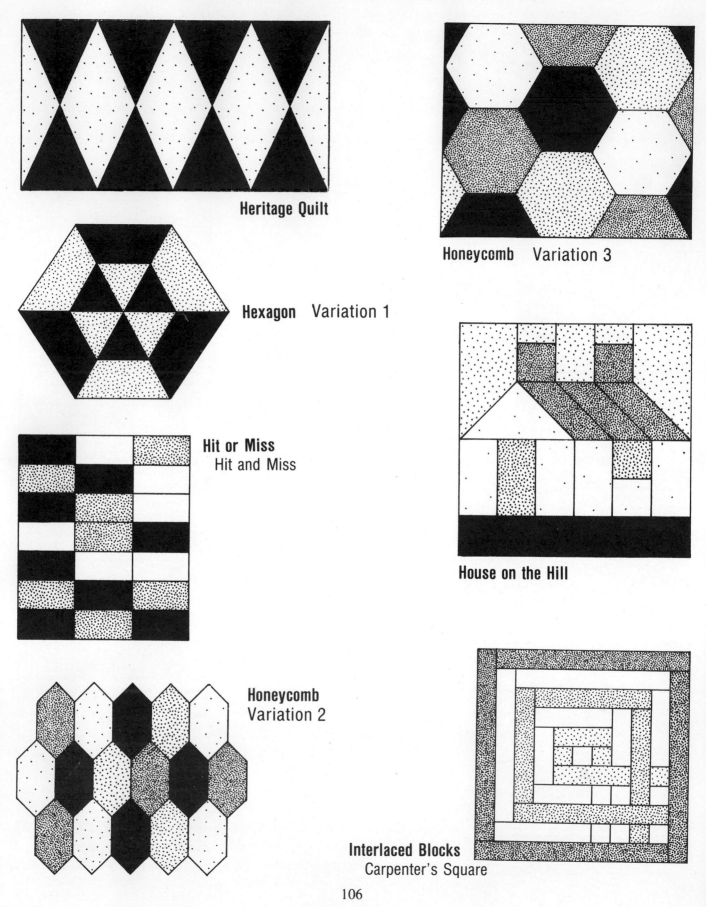

Heritage Quilt

Honeycomb Variation 3

Hexagon Variation 1

Hit or Miss
Hit and Miss

House on the Hill

Honeycomb
Variation 2

Interlaced Blocks
Carpenter's Square

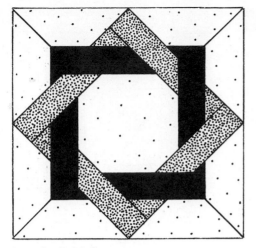

Interlocked Squares

Kansas Dugout

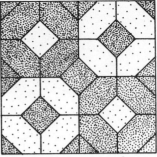

Kite's Tail

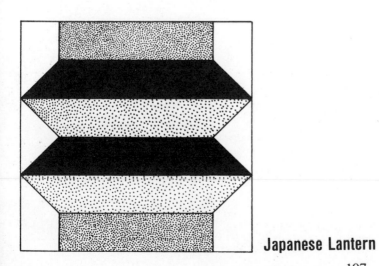

Irish Chain Variation 2
Double Nine-Patch

Leavenworth Nine-Patch

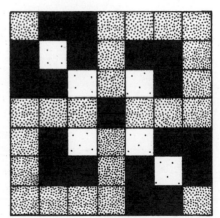

Letter H

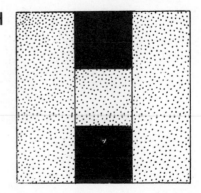

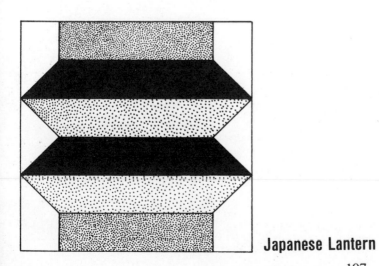

Japanese Lantern

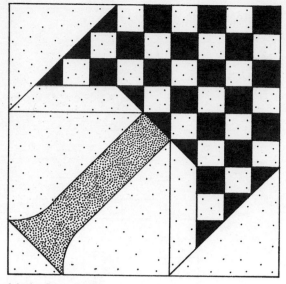

Little Beech Tree

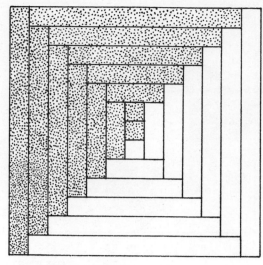

Log Cabin Variation 2
Courthouse Steps

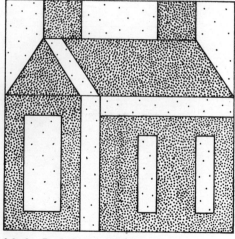

Little Red Schoolhouse

Log Cabin Variation 3

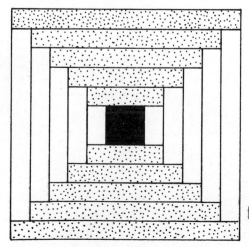

Log Cabin Variation 1
Old-Fashioned Log Cabin

Log Cabin
Variation 4

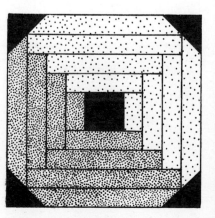

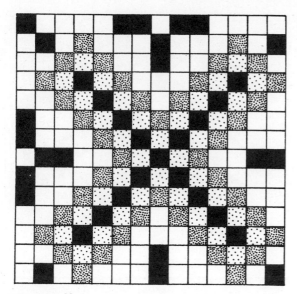

Madam X

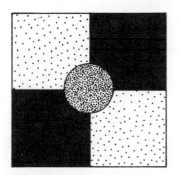

Necktie Variation 1

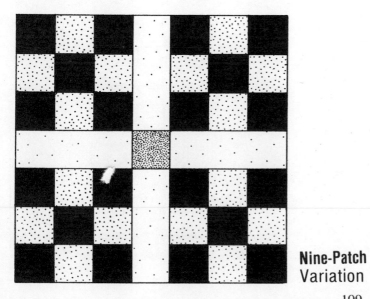

Nine-Patch
Variation 1

Nine-Patch
Variation 3

Nine-Patch
Variation 4

Nine-Patch Chain

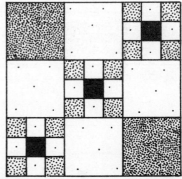

Octagon

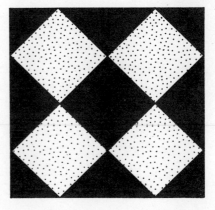

109

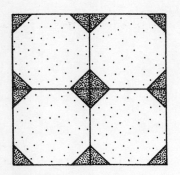

Octagons

Patience Corners

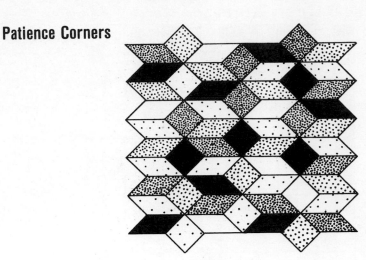

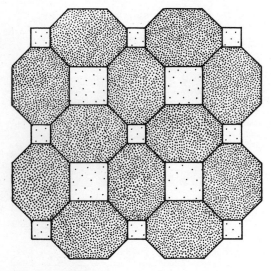

Octagon Tile

Peony

Patience Corner

Pineapple
Chestnut Burr
Church Steps
Maltese Cross, Var. 2

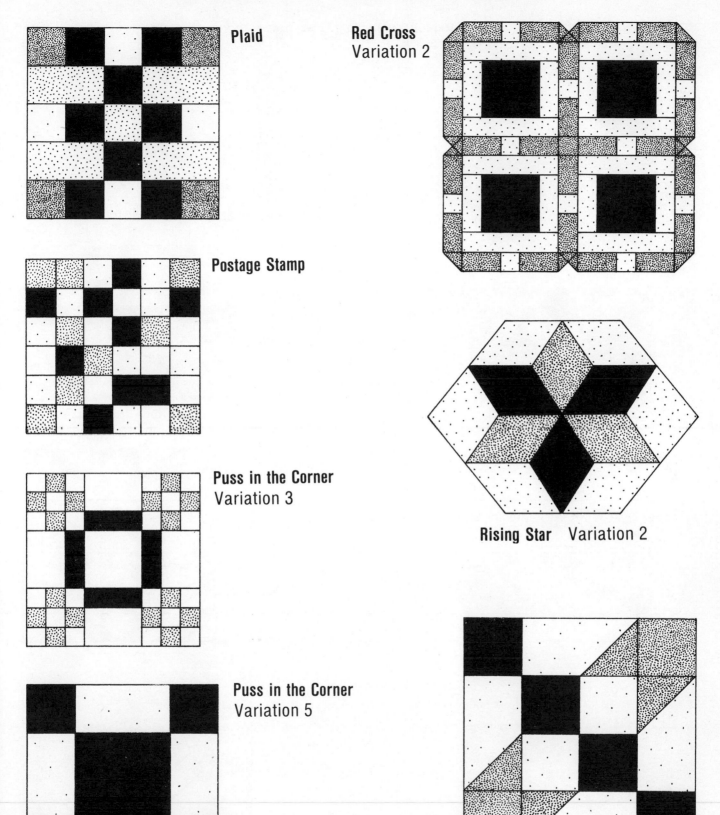

Plaid

Red Cross
Variation 2

Postage Stamp

Puss in the Corner
Variation 3

Rising Star Variation 2

Puss in the Corner
Variation 5

Road to Oklahoma

New Four-Patch

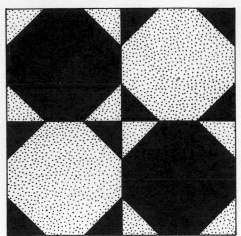

**Robbing Peter to
Pay Paul**
Variation 5

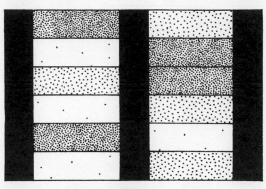

Roman Stripe Variation 1

Rocky Glen
Variation 3

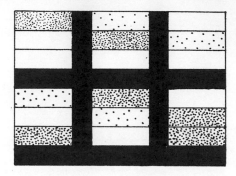

Roman Stripe Variation 2
Roman Square, Var. 1

Roman Cross

Roman Wall

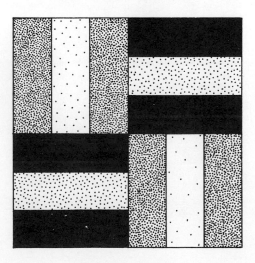

Roman Square
Variation 2
Roman Stripe Zigzag

Sawtooth
Variation 7

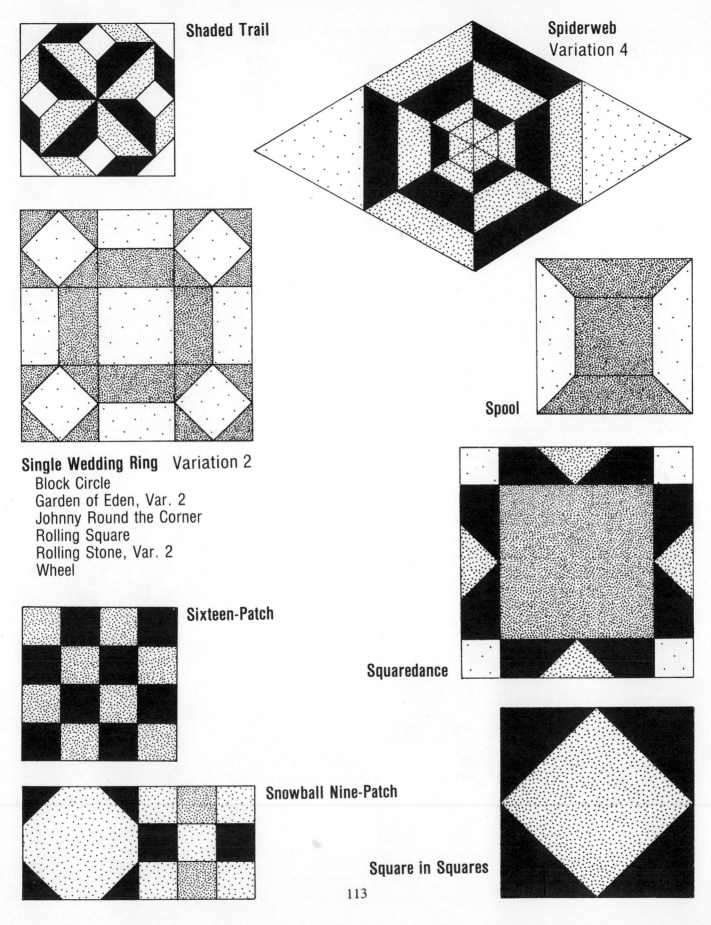

Shaded Trail

Spiderweb
Variation 4

Spool

Single Wedding Ring Variation 2
   Block Circle
   Garden of Eden, Var. 2
   Johnny Round the Corner
   Rolling Square
   Rolling Stone, Var. 2
   Wheel

Squaredance

Sixteen-Patch

Snowball Nine-Patch

Square in Squares

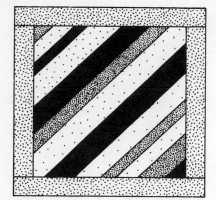

Square with Stripes

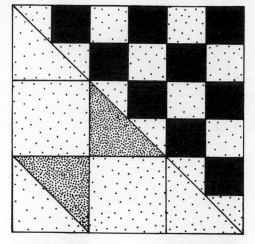

Steps to the Altar
Variation 2

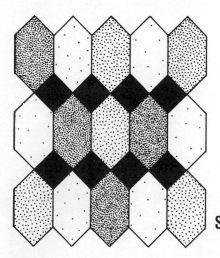

Stained Glass
Church Window

Streak O'Lightning

Strips and Squares
Strip Squares

Stepping Stones
Variation 2
Arrowheads, Var. 2

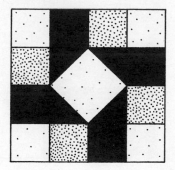

Susannah
Variation 1

114

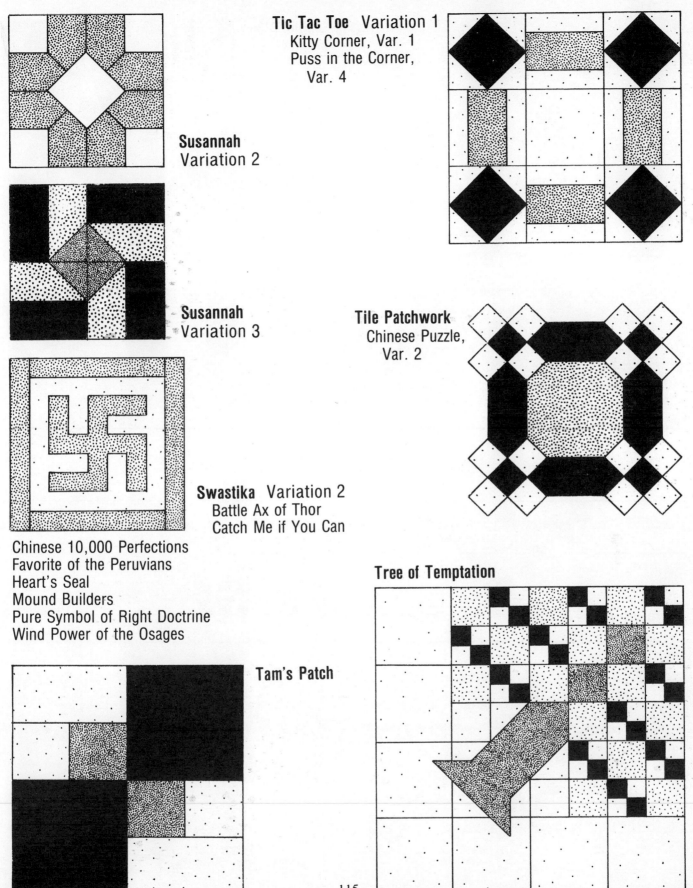

Susannah Variation 2

Susannah Variation 3

Swastika Variation 2
Battle Ax of Thor
Catch Me if You Can

Chinese 10,000 Perfections
Favorite of the Peruvians
Heart's Seal
Mound Builders
Pure Symbol of Right Doctrine
Wind Power of the Osages

Tam's Patch

Tic Tac Toe Variation 1
Kitty Corner, Var. 1
Puss in the Corner,
Var. 4

Tile Patchwork
Chinese Puzzle,
Var. 2

Tree of Temptation

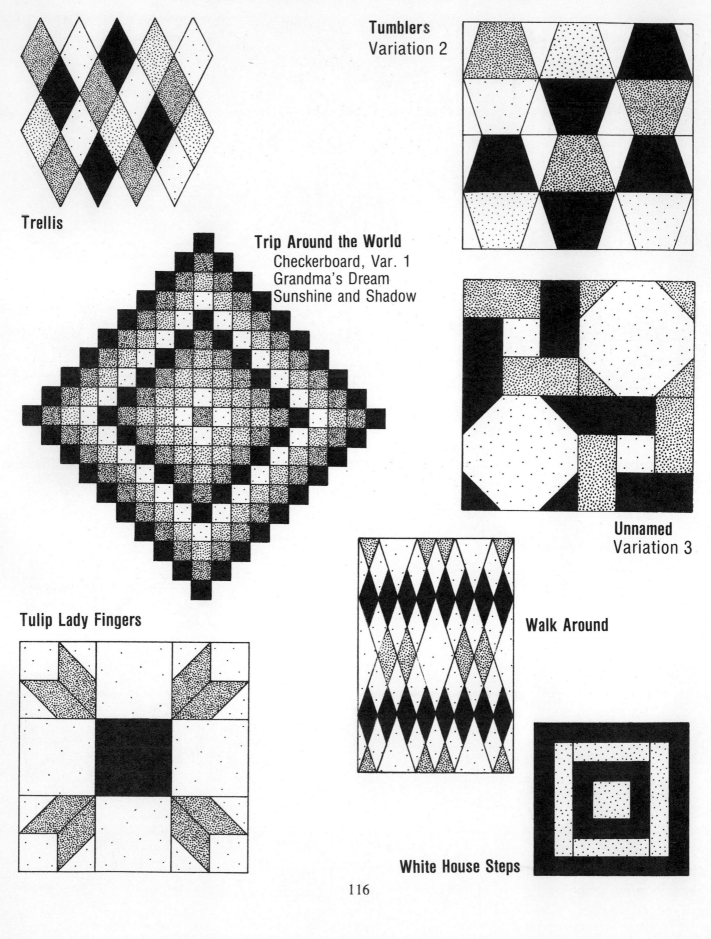

Trellis

Tumblers
Variation 2

Trip Around the World
Checkerboard, Var. 1
Grandma's Dream
Sunshine and Shadow

Unnamed
Variation 3

Tulip Lady Fingers

Walk Around

White House Steps

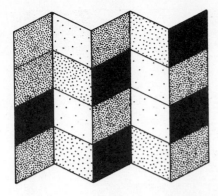

Zigzag
Variation 2
Snake Fence, Var. 2

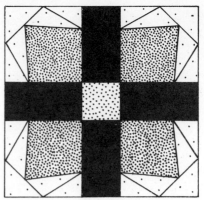

Star and Cross Variation 3

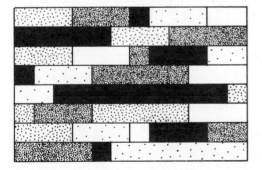

Zigzag
Variation 3

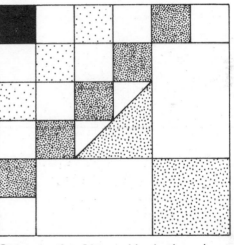

Steps to the Altar Variation 1

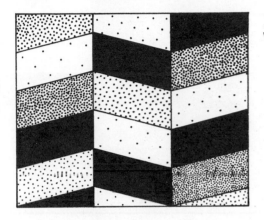

Zigzag Block

SUPPLEMENT

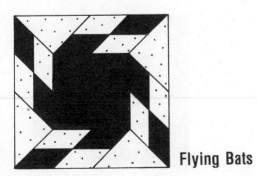

Flying Bats

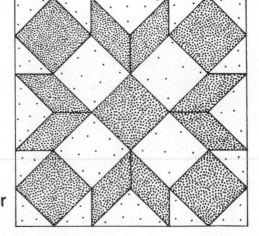

Swing in the Center
Variation 2

BIBLIOGRAPHY

Bicentennial Quilt Book, McCall's Needlework & Crafts, Editorial Director, Rosemary McMurtry, McCall Pattern Co., New York, 1975.

ERICSON, HELEN M., *Helen's Book of Basic Quiltmaking,* Groh Printing Co., Emporia, Kansas, 1973.

FINLEY, RUTH E., *Old Patchwork Quilts,* Charles T. Branford Co., Newton Centre, Mass., c. 1929, reprinted 1970.

The Foxfire Book, Editor, Eliot Wigginton, Anchor Books/Doubleday, Garden City, N.Y., 1972.

GRAFTON, CAROL BELANGER, *Traditional Patchwork Patterns,* Dover Publications, Inc., New York, 1974.

GREEN, SYLVIA, *Patchwork for Beginners,* Watson-Guptill Publications, New York, 1972.

GUTCHEON, BETH, *The Perfect Patchwork Primer,* Penguin Books Inc., Baltimore, 1973.

Heirloom Quilts, McCall's Needlework and Crafts, Editorial Director, Rosemary McMurtry, McCall Pattern Co., 1974.

HINSON, DOLORES, A., *A Quilter's Companion,* Arco Publishing, Inc., New York, 1973.

HOLSTEIN, JONATHAN, *American Pieced Quilts,* Viking Press, New York, 1972.

LARSEN, JUDITH LA BELLE & GULL, CAROL WAUGH, *The Patchwork Quilt Design & Coloring Book,* Butterick Publishing, New York, 1977.

LITHGOW, MARILYN, *Quiltmaking & Quiltmakers,* Funk & Wagnalls, New York, 1974.

MAHLER, CELINE BLANCHARD, *Once Upon a Quilt,* Van Nostrand Reinhold Co., New York, 1973.

The McCall's Book of Quilts, Editors of McCall's Needlework & Crafts Publications, Simon & Schuster/The McCall Pattern Company, New York, 1975.

McKIM, RUBY SHORT, *One Hundred and One Patchwork Patterns,* Dover Publications, Inc., New York, 1962.

Mountain Artizans, An Exhibition of Patchwork and Quilting, Museum of Art, Rhode Island School of Design, Providence, 1970.

Mrs. Danner's Fifth Quilt Book, Editor, Helen M. Ericson, Groh Printing Co., Emporia, Kansas, 1972.

Mrs. Danner's Quilts, Books 1 and 2 combined, Editor, Helen M. Ericson, Groh Printing Co., Emporia, Kansas, 1971.

Mrs. Danner's Quilts, Books 3 and 4 combined, Editor, Helen M. Ericson, Groh Printing Co., Emporia, Kansas, 1973.

ORLOFSKY, PATSY & MYRON, *Quilts in America,* McGraw-Hill Book Co., New York, 1974.

PETO, FLORENCE, *Quilts & Coverlets,* Chanticleer Press, New York, 1949.

Quilter's Newsletter Magazine, Editor-Bonnie Leman, Leman Publications, Inc., Denver.

Quilt World, Editor-Barbara Hall Pedersen.

150 Years of American Quilts, The University of Kansas Museum of Art, Lawrence, Kansas, 1973.

INDEX

AIRCRAFT, 30
AIRPLANE, 98
ALBUM
  Variation 1, 64
  Variation 2, 64
  Variation 3, 98
  Variation 4, 30
  Variation 5, 30
ALBUM PATCH, 98
ALICE'S FAVORITE, 2
ALL HALLOWS, 2
ALL KINDS, 99
ALWAYS FRIENDS, 60
AMETHYST, 27
ANTIQUE SHOP TULIP, 64
ANVIL, 30
ARABIC LATTICE, 64
ARABIAN STAR, 7
ARKANSAS SNOWFLAKE, 2
ARKANSAS TRAVELLER, 2

AROUND THE WORLD, 54
ARROWHEADS
  Variation 1, 64
  Variation 2, 114
ARROW STAR
  Variation 1, 2
  Variation 2, 23
ASTER, 56
AUNT ELIZA'S STAR, 2
AUNT SUKEY'S CHOICE, 64
AUTUMN LEAF, 96
AUTUMN TINTS, 98

BABY BLOCKS
  Variation 1, 98
  Variation 2, 65
BABY BUNTING, 54
BACHELOR'S PUZZLE
  Variation 1, 98

  Variation 2, 98
BAILEY NINE-PATCH, 57
BALKAN PUZZLE, 50
BARBARA FRIETCHIE STAR, 30
BARN DOOR, 89
BARN RAISING, 30
BARRISTER'S BLOCK, 30
BASEBALL, 54
BASKET OF LILIES
  Variation 1, 65
  Variation 2, 65
BASKET OF SCRAPS, 65
BASKET OF TRIANGLES, 30
BASKET OF TULIPS,
  Variation 1, 65
  Variation 2, 65
BASKETS, 65
BASKETWEAVE, 99
BATTLE AX OF THOR, 115
BATTLEGROUNDS, 37

BAY LEAF, 54
BEAR'S FOOT, 65
BEAR'S PAW
  Variation 1, 73
  Variation 2, 39
  Variation 3, 65
BEAR'S TRACK
  Variation 1, 65
  Variation 2, 65
BEAR TRACKS
  Variation 1, 65
  Variation 2, 65
BEAUTIFUL STAR, 2
BEGGAR'S BLOCK, 66
BEGGAR'S BLOCKS, 99
BIRDS IN AIR
  Variation 1, 31
  Variation 2, 31
  Variation 3, 31
BIRD'S NEST, 66
BLACKFORD'S BEAUTY, 66
BLAZING STAR
  Variation 1, 3
  Variation 2, 3
  Variation 3, 15
BLAZING SUN, 3
BLINDMAN'S FANCY, 31
BLOCK CIRCLE, 113
BLOCKS AND STARS, 66
BOUQUET IN A FAN, 3
BOUTONNIERE, 21
BOW, 31
BOW KNOT, 66
BOWS AND ARROWS, 60
BOWTIE, 104
BOX, 99
BOX AND STAR, 3
BOXED Ts, 66
BOXES
  Variation 1, 98
  Variation 2, 32
BRACED STAR, 66
BRICKS, 99
BRICK WALL, 99
BRICKWORK, 99
BRIDAL STAIRWAY, 99
BROKEN DISHES, 32
BROWN, 32
BROWN GOOSE, 32
BRUNSWICK STAR
  Variation 1, 4
  Variation 2, 23
BULL'S EYE, 75
BURGOYNE'S QUILT, 99
BURGOYNE SURROUNDED, 99
BURNHAM SQUARE, 67
BUTTERCUP, 54
BUTTERFLY
  Variation 1, 67
  Variation 2, 67
BUTTONS AND BOWS, 32

CACTUS BASKET
  Variation 1, 67
  Variation 2, 65
CACTUS FLOWER, 32
CAESER'S CROWN, 3
CAKESTAND, 32
CALIFORNIA OAK LEAF, 105
CALIFORNIA STAR
  Variation 1, 4
  Variation 2, 4
CAPITAL T, 47

CAPTAIN'S WHEEL, 67
CARD TRICK, 33
CARPENTER'S SQUARE, 106
CARPENTER'S WHEEL
  Variation 1, 25
  Variation 2, 4
CASTLE IN AIR, 33
CASTLE WALL, 27
CATCH ME IF YOU CAN, 115
CATHEDRAL WINDOW, 58
CATS AND MICE
  Variation 1, 67
  Variation 2, 66
CAT'S CRADLE, 33
CENTURY
  Variation 1, 100
  Variation 2, 33
CENTURY OF PROGRESS, 100
CHAIN, 67
CHAIN AND HOURGLASS, 67
CHAINED FIVE-PATCH, 100
CHAINED STAR, 4
CHECKERBOARD
  Variation 1, 116
  Variation 2, 100
  Variation 3, 100
CHECKERBOARD SKEW, 68
CHERRY BASKET
  Variation 1, 33
  Variation 2, 33
CHESTNUT BURR, 110
CHEVRON, 40
CHICAGO STAR, 5
CHILDREN OF ISRAEL, 68
CHILDREN'S DELIGHT, 100
CHIMNEY SWALLOWS, 5
CHIMNEY SWEEP, 101
CHINESE COIN, 89
CHINESE PUZZLE
  Variation 1, 68
  Variation 2, 115
CHINESE STAR, 5
CHINESE 10,000 PERFECTIONS, 115
CHIPS AND WHETSTONES
  Variation 1, 5
  Variation 2, 5
  Variation 3, 5
CHRISTIAN CROSS, 101
CHRISTMAS STAR
  Variation 1, 6
  Variation 2, 68
CHRISTMAS TREE, 33
CHURCH STEPS, 110
CHURCH WINDOW, 114
CHURN DASH
  Variation 1, 68
  Variation 2, 68
CIRCLE CROSS, 54
CIRCLING SWALLOWS, 9
CIRCULAR SAW, 54
CITY SQUARE, 34
CLAMSHELL, 54
CLAWS, 68
CLAY'S CHOICE, 69
CLIMBING ROSE, 39
CLOVER BLOSSOM, 69
CLOWN'S CHOICE, 40
CLUSTER OF STARS, 6
COARSEWOVEN
  Variation 1, 103
  Variation 2, 101
COFFIN STAR, 101
COLUMBIA PUZZLE 6

COLUMBIA STAR, 6
COLUMNS, 6
COMBINATION STAR, 69
COMPASS
  Variation 1, 24
  Variation 2, 57
  Variation 3, 59
CONTRARY WIFE, 101
CORN AND BEANS
  Variation 1, 35
  Variation 2, 34
CORNER POSTS, 101
COTTON REEL, 34
COUNTRY CROSSROADS, 55
COUNTRY HUSBAND, 55
COUNTRY ROADS, 101
COUNTY FAIR, 83
COURTHOUSE SQUARE, 101
COURTHOUSE STEPS, 108
COXEY'S CAMP, 102
CRAZY ANN
  Variation 1, 34
  Variation 2, 69
CRAZY HOUSE, 69
CRIMSON RAMBLER, 42
CROSS
  Variation 1, 34
  Variation 2, 102
CROSS AND CROWN
  Variation 1, 69
  Variation 2, 70
  Variation 3, 65
  Variation 4, 70
CROSSED CANOES, 34
CROSSES AND LOSSES, 34
CROSSROADS, 55
CROSS UPON A CROSS, 70
CROSS UPON CROSS, 76
CROSS WITHIN A CROSS, 70
CROW FOOT, 70
CROWN AND CROSS, 70
CROWN AND THORNS, 70
CROWNED CROSS
  Variation 1, 70
  Variation 2, 76
CROWN OF THORNS, 70
CROW'S FOOT
  Variation 1, 73
  Variation 2, 85
  Variation 3, 50
  Variation 4, 70
CUBEWORK, 98
CUPID'S ARROWPOINT, 102
CUTSGLASS DISH, 50

DAVID AND GOLIATH
  Variation 1, 75
  Variation 2, 71
  Variation 3, 71
DELECTABLE MOUNTAINS
  Variation 1, 71
  Variation 2, 71
  Variation 3, 71
DESERT ROSE
  Variation 1, 67
  Variation 2, 65
DEVIL'S CLAWS
  Variation 1, 32
  Variation 2, 70
DEVIL'S PUZZLE
  Variation 1, 71
  Variation 2, 72
DIAMOND STAR

Variation 1, 6
Variation 2, 7
DIVIDED STAR, 13
DOE AND DARTS, 75
DOGWOOD BLOSSOMS, 72
DOLLY MADISON'S STAR, 28
DOLLY MADISON'S WORKBOX
Variation 1, 57
Variation 2, 57
DOMINO
Variation 1, 102
Variation 2, 102
DOMINO AND SQUARE, 102
DOMINO AND SQUARES, 72
DOUBLE IRISH CHAIN, 102
DOUBLE IRISH CROSS, 102
DOUBLE MONKEY WRENCH, 89
DOUBLE NINE-PATCH, 107
DOUBLE PEONY, 103
DOUBLE PYRAMID, 35
DOUBLE SAWTOOTH, 35
DOUBLE SQUARE
Variation 1, 72
Variation 2, 91
DOUBLE STAR, 25
DOUBLE T
Variation 1, 35
Variation 2, 47
DOUBLE TULIP, 64
DOUBLE WEDDING RING, 55
DOUBLE X
Variation 1, 72
Variation 2, 34
DOUBLE Z, 32
DOVE AT THE WINDOW, 7
DOVE IN THE WINDOW
Variation 1, 35
Variation 2, 72
Variation 3, 51
DRESDEN PLATE
Variation 1, 56
Variation 2, 55
Variation 3, 55
DRUNKARD'S PATH
Variation 1, 55
Variation 2, 55
Variation 3, 55
Variation 4, 56
DUCK AND DUCKLING, 34
DUCK AND DUCKLINGS, 35
DUCK PADDLE, 71
DUCK'S FOOT, 73
DUCK'S FOOT IN THE MUD
Variation 1, 73
Variation 2, 65
DUSTY MILLER, 73
DUTCHMAN'S PUZZLE, 35
DUTCH MILL, 73
DUTCH ROSE, 7
DUTCH TILE, 7
DUTCH WINDMILL, 35

EASTERN STAR
Variation 1, 16
Variation 2, 27
ECCENTRIC STAR
Variaion 1, 73
Variation 2, 7
ECCLESIASTICAL, 103
ECONOMY PATCH, 103
EIGHT HANDS ROUND, 36
Variation 1, 36
Variation 2, 117

EIGHT-POINT STAR, 16
EIGHT-POINTED STAR
Variation 1, 23
Variation 2, 7
Variation 3, 28
ENDLESS CHAIN, 12
ENGLISH IVY, 69
ENIGMA STAR, 8
EVEING STAR
Variation 1, 8
Variation 2, 8
Variation 3, 8
Variation 4, 21
E-Z QUILT, 73

FALLING STAR, 9
FALLING TIMBER, 55
FALLING TIMBERS, 59
FAN, 56
FAN MILL
Variation 1, 50
Variation 2, 85
FANNIE'S FAN
Variation 1, 73
Variation 2, 74
FANNY'S FAN
Variation 1, 56
Variation 2, 71
FARMER'S DAUGHTER, 74
FARMER'S PUZZLE, 66
FAVORITE OF THE PERUVIANS, 115
FEATHERED STAR
Variation 1, 8
Variation 2, 8
FEATHER STAR, 8
FENCE RAIL, 103
FERRIS WHEEL, 103
54-40 OR FIGHT, 96
FINEWOVEN
Variation 1, 103
Variation 2, 101
FISH BLOCK, 9
FIVE-PATCH STAR, 89
FIVE-POINTED STAR, 9
FLAGS AND SHIPS, 36
FLOCK, 36
FLOCK OF GEESE, 31
FLO'S FAN, 56
FLOWER BASKET, 33
FLOWER GARDEN, 105
FLOWER POT
Variation 1, 74
Variation 2, 92
Variation 3, 36
FLOWERS IN A BASKET, 74
FLOWER STAR
Variation 1, 9
Variation 2, 22
FLOWING RIBBON, 74
FLUTTER WHEELS
Variation 1, 50
Variation 2, 85
FLY
Variation 1, 50
Variation 2, 85
FLYFOOT
Variation 1, 71
Variation 2, 72
FLYING BAT, 9
FLYING BATS, 117
FLYING BIRD, 36
FLYING BIRDS, 31
FLYING CLOUDS

Variation 1, 74
Variation 2, 74
FLYING DARTS, 75
FLYING DUTCHMAN
Variation 1, 75
Variation 2, 39
Variation 3, 36
FLYING GEESE
Variation 1, 31
Variation 2, 75
FLYING SAUCER, 9
FLYING SQUARES, 103
FLYING STAR, 9
FLYING SWALLOW, 9
FLYING X, 40
FOLLOW THE LEADER, 34
FOOL'S PUZZLE
Variation 1, 56
Variation 2, 56
FOOT, 85
FORBIDDEN FRUIT, 36
FORBIDDEN FRUIT TREE, 36
FOREST PATH, 39
FORMOSA TEA LEAF, 10
FOUR BIRDS, 24
FOUR DARTS, 75
FOUR FROGS, 74
FOUR-H CLUB, 103
FOUR LITTLE BASKETS, 75
FOUR LITTLE FANS, 54
FOUR-PATCH
Variation 1, 103
Variation 2, 104
Variation 3, 98
FOUR-POINT, 2
FOUR-POINTED STAR, 15
FOUR-SQUARE, 104
FOUR STARS, 12
FOUR Ts, 37
FOUR WINDS, 24
FOUR X, 37
FOUR-X STAR, 89
FOX AND GEESE, 34
FREE TRADE BLOCK, 51
FRENCH BOUQUET, 105
FRENCH STAR, 10
FRIENDSHIP CHAIN, 60
FRIENDSHIP KNOT, 75
FRIENDSHIP RING, 56
FRIENDSHIP SQUARE, 104
FRIENDSHIP STAR
Variation 1, 10
Variation 2, 10
FRUIT BASKET
Variation 1, 37
Variation 2, 31
FULL-BLOWN TULIP
Variation 1, 60
Variation 2, 56
FUNDAMENTAL NINE-PATCH, 104

GARDEN MAZE, 104
GARDEN OF EDEN
Variation 1, 75
Variation 2, 113
GEESE IN FLIGHT, 37
GENTLEMAN'S BOWTIE, 104
GENTLEMAN'S FANCY, 38
GEOMETRIC STAR, 10
GEORGETOWN CIRCLE
Variation 1, 70
Variation 2, 10
GEORGETOWN CIRCLES, 37

GLORIFIED NINE-PATCH, 57
GOLDEN GATE, 104
GOLDEN GATES, 50
GOLDEN GLOW
  Variation 1, 60
  Variation 2, 105
GOLDEN STAIRS, 37
GOLDEN WEDDING RING, 27
GOLDFISH, 9
GOLGOTHA
  Variation 1, 76
  Variation 2, 70
GOOSE IN THE POND
  Variation 1, 38
  Variation 2, 95
GOOSE TRACKS
  Variation 1, 65
  Variation 2, 71
  Variation 3, 76
GRANDMA'S DREAM, 116
GRANDMA'S GARDEN, 105
GRANDMA'S RED AND WHITE, 105
GRANDMOTHER'S BASKET, 76
GRANDMOTHER'S CHOICE
  Variation 1, 96
  Variation 2, 89
GRANDMOTHER'S CROSS, 76
GRANDMOTHER'S DREAM 76
GRANDMOTHER'S FAN, 56
GRANDMOTHER'S FAVORITE, 38
GRANDMOTHER'S FLOWER GARDEN,
  105
GRANDMOTHER'S PINWHEEL, 38
GRANNY'S FLOWER GARDEN, 105
GRAPE BASKET, 38
GRECIAN, 77
GRECIAN DESIGN, 77
GREEK CROSS
  Variation 1, 80
  Variation 2, 76
  Variation 3, 77
GRETCHEN, 38
GREY GOOSE, 32
GUIDING STAR, 10

HAND, 105
HAND OF FRIENDSHIP
  Variation 1, 73
  Variation 2, 65
HANDY ANDY
  Variation 1, 38
  Variation 2, 77
  Variation 3, 77
  Variation 4, 34
  Variation 5, 35
  Variation 6, 75
HANGING DIAMOND, 105
HARIEQUIN STAR, 11
HARRY'S STAR, 69
HARVEST STAR, 19
HARVEST SUN, 19
HAYES' CORNER, 77
HEARTS AND GIZZARDS, 56
HEART'S DESIRE, 77
HEART'S SEAL, 115
HEAVENLY STAIRS, 98
HEAVENLY STARS, 11
HEAVENLY STEPS, 98
HEN AND CHICKENS
  Variation 1, 34
  Variation 2, 77
HENRY OF THE WEST, 69
HENS AND CHICKENS, 35

HERITAGE QUILT, 106
HEXAGON
  Variation 1, 106
  Variation 2, 103
HILL AND VALLEY, 38
HIT AND MISS, 106
HIT OR MISS, 106
HOLE IN THE BARN DOOR, 89
HONEYCOMB
  Variation 1, 105
  Variation 2, 106
  Variation 3, 106
HONEY'S CHOICE, 50
HOPE OF HARTFORD, 38
HOPSCOTCH, 11
HOSANNA, 43
HOURGLASS
  Variation 1, 78
  Variation 2, 50
HOUSE ON THE HILL, 106
HOVERING BIRDS, 39
HUNTER'S STAR, 11

ICE CREAM BOWL, 39
ILLINOIS TURKEY TRACK, 65
IMPROVED NINE-PATCH
  Variation 1, 57
  Variation 2, 91
INDIANA PUZZLE, 78
INDIAN HATCHET
  Variation 1, 78
  Variation 2, 78
  Variation 3, 51
INDIAN MEADOWS
  Variation 1, 78
  Variation 2, 39
INDIAN PLUMES, 39
INDIAN SUMMER, 58
INDIAN TRAILS
  Variation 1, 39
  Variation 2, 37
INDIAN WEDDING RING, 58
INTERLACED BLOCKS, 106
INTERLOCKED SQUARES, 107
IOWA STAR, 11
IRISH CHAIN
  Variation 1, 78
  Variation 2, 107
IRISH PUZZLE, 39

JACK IN THE BOX, 79
JACK IN THE PULPIT, 91
JACKSON'S STAR
  Variation 1, 11
  Variation 2, 69
JACKSON STAR, 12
JACOB'S LADDER
  Variation 1, 79
  Variation 2, 79
JAPANESE LANTERN, 107
JOB'S TEARS, 12
JOB'S TROUBLES
  Variation 1, 105
  Variation 2, 2
JOHNNY ROUND THE CORNER, 113
JOSEPH'S COAT
  Variation 1, 79
  Variation 2, 79
JOSEPH'S NECKTIE, 104
KALEIDOSCOPE
  Variation 1, 12
  Variation 2, 39
  Variation 3, 39

KANSAS DUGOUT, 107
KANSAS TROUBLE
  Variation 1, 39
  Variation 2, 40
KANSAS TROUBLES, 12
KATHY'S RAMBLE
  Variation 1, 50
  Variation 2, 85
KEY WEST STAR, 12
KING DAVID'S CROWN
  Variation 1, 12
  Variation 2, 79
KING'S CROWN
  Variation 1, 80
  Variation 2, 80
  Variation 3, 80
KING'S STAR
  Variation 1, 12
  Variation 2, 24
KITE, 2
KITE'S TAIL, 107
KITTY CORNER
  Variation 1, 115
  Variation 2, 86

LADIES' DELIGHT, 80
LADY OF THE LAKE
  Variation 1, 42
  Variation 2, 40
  Variation 3, 43
LAFAYETTE ORANGE PEEL, 57
LAWYER'S PUZZLE, 30
LAZY DAISY
  Variation 1, 56
  Variation 2, 13
LEAPFROG, 80
LEAVENWORTH NINE-PATCH, 107
LEAVENWORTH STAR, 13
LEMON STAR
  Variation 1, 23
  Variation 2, 13
  Variation 3, 3
LE MOYNE STAR
  Variation 1, 23
  Variation 2, 13
LETTER H, 107
LETTER X, 40
LIBERTY STAR, 13
LIGHT AND SHADOWS, 13
LIGHTNING STRIPS, 40
LILY, 80
LILY DESIGN, 65
LILY OF THE FIELD, 80
LINCOLN'S PLATFORM, 89
LITTLE BEECH TREE, 108
LITTLE GIANT, 81
LITTLE LOST SHIP, 12
LITTLE RED SCHOOLHOUSE, 108
LOG CABIN
  Variation 1, 108
  Variation 2, 108
  Variation 3, 108
  Variation 4, 108
LOG CABIN STAR, 13
LONDON SQUARE, 34
LONE STAR
  Variation 1, 16
  Variation 2, 16
LOST SHIPS
  Variation 1, 40
  Variation 2, 51
LOVE KNOT, 89
LOVE RING, 57

LOVER'S KNOT, 68
LUCINDA'S STAR, 14
LUCKY STAR, 16

MADAM X, 109
MAGNOLIA BUD, 81
MALTESE CROSS
  Variation 1, 40
  Variation 2, 110
MANY-POINTED STAR, 14
MAPLE LEAF
  Variation 1, 81
  Variation 2, 81
  Variation 3, 27
MARE'S NEST, 81
MARINER'S COMPASS, 14
MARTHA WASHINGTON'S FLOWER
  GARDEN, 105
MARTHA WASHINGTON STAR, 14
MARYLAND BEAUTY, 40
MARY TENNEY GRAY TRAVEL CLUB
  PATCH, 81
MELON PATCH, 57
MEMORY BLOCK, 81
MEMORY CHAIN, 82
MEMORY WREATH, 70
MERRY GO ROUND, 41
MEXICAN CROSS, 82
MEXICAN ROSE, 14
MEXICAN STAR
  Variation 1, 14
  Variation 2, 71
MILKY WAY, 82
MILL WHEEL
  Variation 1, 50
  Variation 2, 59
MISSOURI BEAUTY, 57
MISSOURI PUZZLE
  Variation 1, 82
  Variation 2, 82
MISSOURI STAR, 14
MIXED T, 37
MODERNISTIC TRUMPET VINE, 82
MODERN STAR, 15
MOLLIE'S CHOICE, 79
MONKEY WRENCH
  Variation 1, 68
  Variation 2, 89
  Variation 3, 78
  Variation 4, 82
MORNING STAR
  Variation 1, 15
  Variation 2, 15
  Variation 3, 15
MOSAIC, 105
MOTHER'S DREAM, 76
MOTHER'S FANCY STAR, 83
MOUND BUILDERS, 115
MOUNTAIN MEADOWS, 78
MRS. CLEVELAND'S CHOICE, 83
MRS. MORGAN'S CHOICE, 41
MRS. WOLF'S RED BEAUTY, 95

NECKTIE
  Variation 1, 109
  Variation 2, 83
NELSON'S VICTORY, 83
NEW FOUR-PATCH, 111
NEW YORK BEAUTY
  Variation 1, 41
  Variation 2, 41
NEXT-DOOR NEIGHBOR, 41
NIGHT AND DAY, 41

NINE-PATCH
  Variation 1, 109
  Variation 2, 83
  Variation 3, 109
  Variation 4, 109
NINE-PATCH CHAIN, 109
NONESUCH, 57
NORTH CAROLINA STAR, 24
NORTHERN LIGHTS, 15
NORTH STAR, 15
NORTHUMBERLAND STAR
  Variation 1, 83
  Variation 2, 16
NORTH WIND
  Variation 1, 39
  Variation 2, 42
NOSEGAY
  Variation 1, 96
  Variation 2, 84
OCEAN WAVES
  Variation 1, 42
  Variation 2, 42
  Variation 3, 42
OCTAGON, 109
OCTAGONAL STAR
  Variation 1, 7
  Variation 2, 84
OCTAGONS, 110
OCTAGON TILE, 110
ODD FELLOWS' CHAIN, 42
ODD FELLOWS' CROSS
  Variation 1, 16
  Variation 2, 16
ODDS AND ENDS, 57
ODD STAR, 16
OHIO STAR
  Variation 1, 16
  Variation 2, 16
OKLAHOMA STAR, 17
OLD-FASHIONED LOG CABIN, 108
OLD KING COLE'S CROWN, 84
OLD MAID'S PUZZLE, 34
OLD MAID'S RAMBLE
  Variation 1, 39
  Variation 2, 42
  Variation 3, 42
  Variation 4, 43
OLD MILL WHEEL, 59
OLD TIPPECANOE, 43
OLD TIPPECANOE AND TYLER TOO,
  16
OLD WINDMILL, 50
OLIVE'S YELLOW TULIP, 17
1,000 PYRAMIDS, 40
ORANGE PEEL
  Variation 1, 57
  Variation 2, 57
  Variation 3, 57
ORIENTAL STAR
  Variation 1, 17
  Variation 2, 60
ORIOLE WINDOW, 54
ORNATE STAR, 69
OZARK DIAMOND, 17
OZARK STAR, 17
PALM, 43
PALM LEAF
  Variation 1, 43
  Variation 2, 81
PALM LEAVES HOSANNAH!, 43
PANDORA'S BOX, 98
PANSY, 84
PATH THROUGH THE WOODS, 43

PATIENCE CORNER, 110
PATIENCE CORNERS, 110
PATTY'S STAR, 17
PEONY, 110
PERSIAN STAR, 18
PETAL QUILT, 56
PHILADELPHIA PAVEMENT, 84
PHILIPPINES, 18
PICKET FENCE, 101
PICKLE DISH, 58
PIECED PYRAMIDS, 84
PIECED ROSE, 88
PIECED STAR
  Variation 1, 18
  Variation 2, 84
PIERCED STAR, 18
PIERROT'S POM-PON, 56
PIGEON TOES, 84
PILOT'S WHEEL, 58
PINCUSHION, 58
PINEAPPLE, 110
PINE BURR, 85
PINE TREE
  Variation 1, 92
  Vairation 2, 43
  Variation 3, 43
  Variation 4, 44
PINWHEEL
  Variation 1, 50
  Variation 2, 85
PINWHEELS, 85
PINWHEEL SKEW, 85
PINWHEEL STAR, 44
PLAID, 111
POINTING STAR, 18
POLARIS STAR, 9
PONTIAC STAR, 18
POPLAR LEAF, 81
POSTAGE STAMP, 111
PRAIRIE QUEEN
  Variation 1, 85
  Variation 2, 19
PRAIRIE STAR, 19
PREMIUM STAR, 85
PRICKLY PEAR
  Variation 1, 86
  Variation 2, 39
PRIMROSE PATH, 86
PROPELLOR, 86
PULLMAN PUZZLE, 59
PURE SYMBOL OF RIGHT DOCTRINE,
  115
PURPLE CROSS, 19
PUSS IN BOOTS, 86
PUSS IN THE CORNER
  Variation 1, 86
  Variation 2, 86
  Variation 3, 111
  Variation 4, 115
  Variation 5, 111
PUSS 'N' BOOTS, 64
PUZZLED TILE, 91
PYRAMIDS, 47

QUAIL'S NEST, 89
QUEEN CHARLOTTE'S CROWN
  Variation 1, 78
  Variation 2, 39
QUEEN OF THE MAY, 19
QUEEN'S CROWN
  Variation 1, 58
  Variation 2, 58
QUEEN'S PRIDE, 58

RAIL FENCE, 40
RAILROAD, 86
RAILROAD CROSSING
    Variation 1, 44
    Variation 2, 87
RAINBOW TILE, 105
RAMBLER, 42
RAMBLING ROAD
    Variation 1, 39
    Variation 2, 37
RAMBLING ROSE, 39
REBECCA'S FAN, 58
RED BASKET, 87
RED CROSS
    Variation 1, 87
    Variation 2, 111
REEL, 62
REVERSE BASEBALL, 58
RIBBON BORDER, 44
RIBBONS, 44
RIGHT AND LEFT, 87
RING AROUND THE STAR, 19
RISING STAR
    Variation 1, 20
    Variation 2, 111
RISING SUN
    Variation 1, 14
    Variation 2, 17
ROAD TO CALIFORNIA
    Variation 1, 79
    Variation 2, 99
    Variation 3, 87
    Variation 4, 87
ROAD TO OKLAHOMA, 111
ROBBING PETER TO PAY PAUL
    Variation 1, 87
    Variation 2, 59
    Variation 3, 59
    Variation 4, 57
    Variation 5, 112
    Variation 6, 54
ROB PETER TO PAY PAUL
    Variation 1, 59
    Variation 2, 57
ROCK GARDEN, 20
ROCKY GLEN
    Variation 1, 12
    Variation 2, 40
    Variation 3, 112
    Variation 4, 51
ROCKY MOUNTAIN PUZZLE, 88
ROCKY MOUNTAIN ROAD, 41
ROCKY ROAD TO CALIFORNIA, 79
ROCKY ROAD TO DUBLIN, 59
ROCKY ROAD TO KANSAS
    Variation 1, 12
    Variation 2, 20
ROLLING PINWHEEL
    Variation 1, 44
    Variation 2, 45
ROLLING SQUARE, 113
ROLLING STAR
    Variation 1, 20
    Variation 2, 19
    Variation 3, 4
ROLLING STONE
    Variation 1, 90
    Variation 2, 113
ROMAN CROSS, 112
ROMAN SQUARE
    Variation 1, 112
    Variation 2, 112
ROMAN STRIPE

Variation 1, 112
Variation 2, 112
ROMAN STRIPE ZIGZAG, 112
ROMAN WALL, 112
ROSE, 88
ROSE BUD, 45
ROSE DREAM, 92
ROSETTE, 105
ROYAL CROSS, 88
ROYAL STAR
    Variation 1, 20
    Variation 2, 20

SAGE BUD, 92
SAILBOAT, 45
SAILBOATS, 45
ST. GREGORY'S CROSS, 86
ST. LOUIS STAR, 24
SASSAFRAS LEAF, 105
SAWTOOTH
    Variation 1, 8
    Variation 2, 51
    Variation 3, 88
    Variation 4, 51
    Variation 5, 8
    Variation 6, 52
    Variation 7, 112
SCRAP-BAG, 79
SECRET DRAWER, 88
SEESAW, 45
SEVEN SISTERS, 21
SEVEN STARS, 21
SHADED TRAIL, 113
SHADOWS, 88
SHERMAN'S MARCH, 89
SHINING STAR, 14
SHIP, 89
SHIP'S WHEEL, 19
SHOOFLY
    Variation 1, 89
    Variation 2, 16
    Variation 3, 35
    Variation 4, 34
SIGNATURE, 59
SILVER AND GOLD, 24
SINGLE IRISH CHAIN, 104
SINGLE WEDDING RING
    Variation 1, 70
    Variation 2, 113
SISTER'S CHOICE, 89
SIXTEEN-PATCH, 113
SKY ROCKET, 21
SLASH DIAGONAL, 50
SLASHED STAR, 21
SLAVE CHAIN, 12
SMALL BUSINESS, 21
SNAKE FENCE
    Variation 1, 40
    Variation 2, 117
SNOWBALL
    Variation 1, 59
    Variation 2, 59
    Variation 3, 2
    Variation 4, 59
SNOWBALL NINE-PATCH, 113
SNOWBALL WREATH, 60
SNOW CRYSTALS, 11
SOLDIER'S MARCH 37
SOLOMON'S PUZZLE, 55
SPIDERWEB
    Variation 1, 105
    Variation 2, 21
    Variation 3, 22

Variation 4, 113
SPINNER, 45
SPINNING TRIANGLES, 46
SPOOL, 113
SPOOLS, 60
SPRING BEAUTY, 42
SPRINGTIME BLOSSOM, 56
SQUARE AND A HALF, 89
SQUAREDANCE, 113
SQUARE DEAL, 46
SQUARE IN SQUARES, 113
SQUARE WITHIN SQUARES, 89
SQUARE WITH STRIPES, 114
STAINED GLASS, 114
STAR
    Variation 1, 22
    Variation 2, 15
STAR AND BLOCKS, 6
STAR AND CHAINS, 19
STAR AND CONE, 22
STAR AND CRESCENT
    Variation 1, 22
    Variation 2, 22
STAR AND CROSS
    Variation 1, 22
    Variation 2, 82
    Variation 3, 117
STAR AND HEXAGON, 22
STAR AND PLANETS, 22
STAR FLOWER
    Variation 1, 60
    Variation 2, 23
STARLIGHT
    Variation 1, 23
    Variation 2, 23
STAR OF BETHLEHEM, 8
STAR OF HOPE
    Variation 1, 89
    Variation 2, 23
STAR OF LE MOINE
    Variation 1, 23
    Variation 2, 13
STAR OF LE MOYNE
    Variation 1, 23
    Variation 2, 13
STAR OF MANY POINTS, 23
STAR OF NORTH CAROLINA, 24
STAR OF THE EAST
    Variation 1, 23
    Variation 2, 25
    Variation 3, 24
STAR OF THE FOUR WINDS, 22
STAR OF THE WEST
    Variation 1, 24
    Variation 2, 24
    Variation 3, 69
STAR PUZZLE, 30
STARRY LANE, 90
STARS AND SQUARES, 20
STAR SPANGLED BANNER, 89
STAR TULIP
    Variation 1, 24
    Variation 2, 15
STAR UPON STARS, 27
STAR WITHIN A STAR, 25
STEEPLECHASE, 60
STEPPING STONES, 90
STEPPING STONES
    Variation 1, 79
    Variation 2, 114
STEPS TO THE ALTAR
    Variation 1, 117
    Variation 2, 114

STORM AT SEA
   Variation 1, 39
   Variation 2, 90
   Variation 3, 37
STRAWBERRY, 60
STREAK OF LIGHTNING, 40
STREAK O' LIGHTNING, 114
STRING QUILT, 25
STRIPS AND SQUARES, 114
STRIP SQUARES, 114
SUGAR BOWL
   Variation 1, 50
   Variation 2, 85
SUGAR LOAF, 46
SUNBEAM, 25
SUNBURST
   Variation 1, 25
   Variation 2, 25
   Variation 3, 25
   Variation 4, 26
SUN DIAL, 104
SUNFLOWER, 21
SUNSHINE AND SHADOW, 116
SUSANNAH
   Variation 1, 114
   Variation 2, 115
   Variation 3, 115
SUSPENSION BRIDGE, 90
SWALLOW, 46
SWALLOWS IN A WINDOW, 26
SWASTIKA
   Variation 1, 66
   Variation 2, 115
SWEET GUM LEAF, 46
SWING IN THE CENTER
   Variation 1, 90
   Variation 2, 117

TAIL OF BENJAMIN'S KITE, 79
TALL PINE TREE, 46
TAM'S PATCH, 115
TANGLED COBWEBS, 26
TANGLED GARTER, 104
TANGLED TARES, 39
TASSAL PLANT, 90
T-BLOCKS
   Variation 1, 47
   Variation 2, 90
TEA BASKET, 91
TEA LEAF
   Variation 1, 47
   Variation 2, 47
TEMPERANCE TREE, 43
TENNESSEE STAR, 26
TENTS OF ARMAGEDDON, 47
TEXAS, 16
TEXAS ROSE
   Variation 1, 67
   Variation 2, 65
TEXAS STAR, 26
TEXAS TEARS, 12
TEXAS TREASURE
   Variation 1, 67
   Variation 2, 65
THELMA'S CHOICE, 91
THOUSAND PYRAMIDS, 47
THREE CROSSES
   Variation 1, 76
   Variation 2, 70
TIC TAC TOE
   Variation 1, 115
   Variation 2, 86
TILE PATCHWORK, 115

TILE PUZZLE
   Variation 1, 91
   Variation 2, 91
TINY STAR, 22
TIPPECANOE, 34
TIPPECANOE AND TYIER TOO, 16
TIRZAH'S TREASURE, 104
TOAD IN THE PUDDLE
   Variation 1, 91
   Variation 2, 91
TRAIL OF THE COVERED WAGON, 79
TRAVEL STAR, 2
TREE OF LIFE
   Variation 1, 92
   Variation 2, 47
   Variation 3, 33
TREE OF PARADISE
   Variation 1, 47
   Variation 2, 48
   Variation 3, 48
TREE OF TEMPTATION, 115
TRELLIS, 116
TRIANGLE PUZZLE, 48
TRIANGLES, 47
TRIANGLAR TRIANGLES, 48
TRIP AROUND THE WORLD, 116
TRUE LOVER'S BUGGY WHEEL, 61
TRUE LOVER'S KNOT
   Variation 1, 92
   Variation 2, 105
TULIP, 92
TULIP BASKET, 92
TULIP LADY FINGERS, 116
TUMBLERS
   Variation 1, 48
   Variation 2, 116
TUMBLING BLOCKS, 98
TURKEY TRACKS
   Variation 1, 60
   Variation 2, 92
   Variation 3, 92
TURNABOUT T, 92
TWENTY-FOUR TRIANGLES, 48
TWINKLING STAR
   Variation 1, 8
   Variation 2, 22
TWIST AND TURN, 34

UNDERGROUND RAILROAD, 79
UNION SQUARE
   Variation 1, 93
   Variation 2, 93
UNION SQUARES, 49
UNION STAR, 27
UNKNOWN FOUR-PATCH, 49
UNNAMED
   Variation 1, 60
   Variation 2, 61
   Variation 3, 116

VARIABLE STAR, 16
V-BLOCK
   Variation 1, 49
   Variation 2, 49
VICTORIA'S CROWN, 61
VINE OF FRIENDSHIP, 59
VIRGINIA REEL, 20
VIRGINIA'S STAR, 27
VIRGINIA STAR, 27

WAGON TRACKS, 79
WALK AROUND, 116
WANDERING FOOT, 60

WATER MILL, 50
WATER WHEEL
   Variation 1, 50
   Variation 2, 49
   Variation 3, 93
W.C.T.U., 93
WEATHER VANE
   Variation 1, 39
   Variation 2, 93
   Variation 3, 93
WEDDING RING, 55
WEDDING RINGS, 94
WHEEL, 113
WHEEL OF CHANCE, 61
WHEEL OF FORTUNE
   Variation 1, 56
   Variation 2, 99
   Variation 3, 32
   Variation 4, 61
   Variation 5, 61
WHEEL OF MYSTERY, 54
WHIRLIGIG
   Variation 1, 79
   Variation 2, 49
WHIRLWIND, 49
WHITE CROSS, 94
WHITE HOUSE STEPS, 116
WILD GOOSE CHASE
   Variation 1, 50
   Variation 2, 35
   Variation 3, 94
   Variation 4, 50
   Variation 5, 50
WINDBLOWN SQUARE, 50
WINDING WALK, 39
WINDING WAYS, 54
WINDMILL
   Variation 1, 50
   Variation 2, 56
   Variation 3, 94
   Variation 4, 50
   Variation 5, 94
WINDMILL STAR, 27
WIND POWER OF THE OSAGES, 115
WINGED SQUARE
   Variation 1, 50
   Variation 2, 104
WISHING RING, 94
WONDER OF THE WORLD, 61
WORLD'S FAIR
   Variation 1, 95
   Variation 2, 95
WORLD'S PUZZLE, 55
WORLD WITHOUT END, 27
WRENCH, 95

X, 34
X-QUARTET, 95
X-QUISITE, 95

YANKEE PRIDE, 27
YANKEE PUZZLE
   Variation 1, 50
   Variation 2, 51
YOUNG MAN'S FANCY, 95

Z-CROSS, 96
ZIGZAG
   Variation 1, 40
   Variation 2, 117
   Variation 3, 117
ZIGZAG BLOCK, 117
ZIGZAG TILE, 50